4/26/19

FOSTERING HOPE

Living the Dream with My Name on It

Shane Salter

founder, CASA for Children of the District of Columbia

iUniverse, Inc.

New York   Bloomington

Fostering Hope
Living the Dream with My Name on It

Copyright © 2010 Shane Salter

In some instances, I withheld the names of my foster parents and relatives
for privacy's sake. All episodes that appear in this book are real and
accurate and are based on my experience, research, and interviews.

iUniverse books may be ordered through booksellers or by contacting:

iUniverse
1663 Liberty Drive
Bloomington, IN 47403
www.iuniverse.com
1-800-Authors (1-800-288-4677)

ISBN: 978-1-4502-5593-6 (pbk)
ISBN: 978-1-4502-5594-3 (cloth)
ISBN: 978-1-4502-5595-0 (ebk)

Printed in the United States of America

Library of Congress Control Number: 2010913485

iUniverse rev. date: 9/16/2010

If you can't fly, then run.
If you can't run, then walk.
If you can't walk, then crawl.
But whatever you do, keep moving.
Dr. Martin Luther King, Jr.

To David, Tiffany, Shane Rico, Brittney,
Courtney, Moyé, and Nigel—
Thank you for your forgiveness and for loving me in spite of me.

Contents

Acknowledgments

I will always love the lord because he heard my cry and never gave up on me. Gloria, how do I express gratitude for your ability to accept me as I am? Thanks for standing by me in spite of me and helping my dreams come true; I will love you forever. My first-born daughter, Tiffany, I learned so many things as a teen dad growing up with up you—your forgiveness of the mistakes I made sustains me. David my oldest son; you continue to reinforce why every child regardless of age, deserves a permanent family. I am so proud of the man you've become. My first son Shane Rico, your life that taught me giving up is never an option. My baby girl Courtney, you are the child my foster mother promised would remind me of the drama I caused her. Never the less, I am so proud of you and your determination to be great. Brittney, I will always believe in you and the promises of tomorrow. Moyé and Nigel, as I nurture the love you have for one another, my determination to ensure siblings of abuse and neglect remain together is reinforced. Pop Moragne, you inspired this book and on behalf of all those who enjoy it, thank you. My baby brother Keith, I love you more than you could ever imagine; never doubt for a minute that my life is dedicated to the relationship we once had until the system designed to protect us, severed the bond that fosters healthy relationships. Dr. Anderson of Michigan State, and Dr. Stewart of the University of Arkansas-Pine Bluff, thank you for using my life to inform emerging social workers regarding the complexity of family dynamics and how those dynamics can influence resilience in children. Dr. Carol Spigner from the University of Pennsylvania, you've been a mentor and source of comfort to my soul; someday I hope you will be proud of a doctorate earned that captures one dream with my name on it.   to children and families. My special friend Narvin, and I do mean "special…" It has been a journey. You're discovering what it takes to be my friend and sticking around anyway- Thanks. Valli Matthews, through you I discovered the purpose for my pain; rest in peace. Senator Mary Landrieu (D LA), you have been an unwavering friend and champion for kids. Thank you for decades of support, visionary leadership and service to our country and families. Secretary of State Hilary Clinton, thank you for the opportunity to support your efforts as First Lady that helped remove the barriers that keep children from finding safe and permanent homes. To the staff and board members of CASA DC, providing the support of my leadership continues to grow a preeminent volunteer driven, advocacy movement on behalf of abused and neglected children. Special thanks to Arika Orozco for your assistance on this project. To my birth parents and grandparents, thank you for giving me life- someday we will be together again. To those I counted on but could not show up for whatever reason, because I know from where my help comes, I forgive you.

Shane Salter

Preface

Studies have documented a relationship between maltreatment of children and subsequent juvenile delinquency and adult criminal behavior, and the literature widely attests to the high risk of children in foster care for such undesirable outcomes (Wiig, Widom, and Tuell 2003). These children's adverse life experiences understandably traumatize them: young people in foster care are between five and eight times as likely as their peers to be hospitalized for a serious psychiatric disorder (Pilowsky and Wu 2007). Indeed, when researchers compare children in foster care to their peers who are not in foster care, young people in child welfare not only think more often about suicide but even actually attempt to take their own lives more often (Pilowsky and Wu 2007). Foster care children and youth not only need us; they *deserve* our very best from us.

According to recent estimates, only about one-third of teen mothers go on to receive a high school diploma after having a child. Less than half of the young men who father children go on to complete school, and those who do are far less likely to pursue additional education. The grim statistics continue: daughters of teen mothers are 22 percent more likely to become teen mothers themselves, while sons of teen mothers are 13 percent more likely to end up in prison. I was determined not to be in that 13 percent.

Motivated by the vision of a better tomorrow, I struggled to be a loving daddy and to keep my daughter, Tiffany, from being among that 22-percent statistic. Because the challenge of overcoming generational struggles with teen pregnancy, neglect, and abandonment is so huge, I felt compelled to share my journey, to tell what it was like to be born to a teenage mother whose hopes and dreams were shattered by her drug addiction and lack of family support, and to explain what it meant for me to realize I would never have the opportunity to be a child—to grow up in a loving family with a stable home to come back to someday.

This is my journey through the child welfare system, a journey as threatening for a child as any dark alley in America. It is the story of how, against all odds, I survived—and emerged more determined than ever to find the dream with my name on it, to succeed, and to give back.

In 2002, as a consultant for the National CASA Association, I was provided the opportunity to realize one of my dreams when I established CASA for Children of DC. CASA DC recruits and trains volunteers called Court Appointed Special Advocates (CASAs) to work with abused and neglected children. The evidence-based CASA DC model employs a rigorous recruitment, screening, training, and supervision process. Our volunteers serve dual functions as (1) special advocates appointed by family court to advocate for youth and most recently as (2) mentors through our separate mentoring program. Once appointed by a family court judge, CASAs in DC become an official part of the judicial proceedings to serve as both advocates for youth in the legal and social systems and mentors who provide structured support for these young people.

A focus in prevention literature is on the efficacy of positive youth development. Positive youth development proposes that every child has talents, strengths, and interests that offer her or him the potential for a bright future (Damon 2004). One evidence-based strategy to effect positive youth development and reduce problem behaviors is mentoring (DuBois and Karcher 2005). Spencer (2006) found that successful mentoring relationships between adults and adolescents involved authenticity, empathy, collaboration, and companionship. A variety of studies have suggested that an average youth in mentoring does about 10 percent better on a variety of psychosocial measures, such as self-esteem, than a similar youth not in mentoring (DuBois et al. 2002; Karcher 2008). Research on the effects of mentoring on foster care youth is virtually nonexistent. Even so, one recent study found that youth in foster care who reported a mentoring relationship during adolescence experienced significantly improved outcomes when compared with non-mentored foster youth (Ahrens et al. 2008).

CASA recognizes the importance of cultural competency to effectively engage our youth and families, and as such, that value is reflected throughout the organization. Matsumoto observed, "Culture is to human behavior as operating systems are to software, often invisible and unnoticed, yet playing an extremely important role in development and operation" A particular culture may seem dramatically different to an outsider, but to the insider, it is like air—pervasive and unconsciously accepted. CASA DC trains volunteers and staff in cultural competency and appropriateness, including sensitivity to issues of race, ethnicity, economic situation, gender, age, disability, language, religion, and sexual identity.

For many years, it was my vision that the nation's capitol have a solid resource of volunteers committed to assuring abused and neglected children in DC's child welfare system, with the presence of caring adults who foster hope, facilitate preparation for adulthood, and heal. It was thrilling when CASA DC and the DC Superior Court ultimately concluded a Memorandum of Understanding in December 2002 to facilitate services for these children and youth. CASA DC recruits and trains volunteers called Court Appointed Special Advocates to (1) serve as a fact-finder for the judge by thoroughly researching the background of the assigned case; (2) speak on behalf of the child in the courtroom, representing his or her best interests; and (3) act as a watchdog for the child for the duration of the case, ensuring that the case is brought to a swift and appropriate conclusion. Building Up Dynamic Determined Youth (BUDDYs) are recruited to serve as mentors for youth in the child welfare system.

CASA DC's core competency lies in the recruitment, screening, training, and supervision of volunteer CASAs whom judges assign to individual abused and neglected young people. Our CASAs work in the natural environments of their mentees. The children and youth we serve are overwhelmingly African-American, but we also serve biracial, Latino, and Caucasian children. These young people's ages range from birth to twenty-one years; most of the youth we serve are older adolescents. We serve slightly more females than males.

Since the founding of CASA DC, our CASAs have served more than eight hundred children and youth. In addition, CASA DC has developed five initiatives that sensitively address the needs of special populations:

The Dual Jacket Initiative serves abused and neglected youth who have been arrested for a crime or convicted of a crime. Many youth in the Dual Jacket Initiative do not receive the support services they would have received if they were only in the child welfare system. CASA volunteers serve as liaisons between family court and juvenile court so that both systems work for the best interests of the youth and not at cross-purposes.

As they age out of the foster care system, foster care youth are at-risk for failure to make a successful transition to independent living. We launched the Preparing Youth for Adulthood Initiative in the fall of 2007 to prepare foster care youth for their transition out of foster care at age twenty-one. CASA and the courts observed that too many youth were aging out of the system without any structure or assistance. In an attempt to reverse that trend, CASA staff and volunteers assist CASA youth to develop and secure permanent connections with caring adults, reside in stable living conditions, and take increasing responsibility for their work and lives.

The Family Treatment Court Initiative works with mothers who, as the result of chemical dependency, face charges of child abuse or neglect. The program is voluntary, and potential candidates undergo screening that includes criminal and child protection background checks, an intake interview, and mental health and physical examinations.

The Lesbian, Gay, Bisexual, and Transgender Initiative provides specialized training to CASA volunteers to enable them to advocate effectively for the special needs of abused and neglected lesbian, gay, bisexual, and transgender (LGBT) foster youth. Identification of LGBT youth is a sensitive and complicated issue; most of them are not comfortable acknowledging their sexuality, because they fear harassment and violence, even when their sexuality is the very source of the abuse and neglect they endure. The LGBT Initiative connects these youth to the therapeutic and supportive services they need in the community and pairs them with CASAs who are sensitive to their situations.

Building Up Dynamic Determined Youth (BUDDYs) Initiative was launched in 2010 with a grant from the Child and Family Services Agency in the District of Columbia to employ methods and techniques that provide various mentoring services, including:

(1) assisting mentees with the development of a written plan with their visions for the future. Each mentor—through conversations,

coaching, and social, cultural, and recreational activities—helps young people to foster a vision of the future.

(2) providing regular contact between the mentor and mentee, through weekly emails and telephone calls, in-person activities with the mentee at least every other week for a total of at least four to six hours per month, and quarterly social/cultural activities that CASA DC sponsors.

(3) involving the family or guardian/caretaker of the mentee. Where possible and appropriate, CASA DC involves the guardian/ caretaker when it matches prospective mentees with mentors.

(4) supporting and recognizing mentees. At one of our quarterly social, cultural, or recreational activities for all mentors and mentees, we give each mentee in the program a certificate of recognition for his or her participation. In addition, we also acknowledge publicly other special and noteworthy accomplishments by mentees in their efforts toward achieving their dreams.

CASA for Children of DC maintains offices at 515 M Street SE, Suite 200, Washington, DC 20003. This location places the agency in one of the census tracts with the highest rates of poverty in the city.

Nestled inside the journey of *Fostering Hope*, which you are about to read, there is a story of trouble and triumph with a message that I believe can be heard by the child within each of us.

Chapter 1
ONE MORE BABY CHILD BORN

One more baby child born, and the busy world just goes on;
His first look at the world is through a broken window pane—
Beyond that ... an alley leading nowhere.
—Valerie Simpson

When I was four years old, I became a parent. My nineteen-year-old mother, Sherry—summoned by her heroin addiction—walked out of our basement apartment in Harlem and left me alone to care for my six-month-old brother, Keith. Because I was the older of her two boys, she had often left me in charge when she had to step out before. I learned early how to prepare bottles and change diapers. People called me "Little Man," and by default, I was the man of the house. I knew to keep the door locked and to never answer it.

The last day I saw my mother, her addiction was raging, and once again, she left our apartment with me in charge. How was I to know it would be the last time I would ever see her? Why didn't she come back? Did she just give up? Did she want us in the first place? For many years, those unanswered questions tormented me. I was much too young to figure it out then. I only hoped to see her one more time.

All I wanted was to remain a little boy and a big brother. Nevertheless, the day my mother walked out, I instantly became a caretaker and parent. Having already given me so much responsibility so early, perhaps my mother, without fully understanding it herself, had been preparing me for the challenge and for the struggles that lay ahead.

I took care of little Keith in the best way I could, but how we managed alone remains a mystery to me. The day our mother departed, there was not much in the house left to eat. After a few days, there was no food at all, Keith cried longer and louder once we were out of milk, and I knew I had to go find some. That meant I had to disobey my mother. Every time she had left us alone, my mom would tell me, "*Never* open the door; *never* leave the house; and *never* let anybody in." But instinctively, I knew I had to ignore her instructions that time, and I headed out the door in search of food, wearing nothing but a dirty diaper, because I'd never been potty-trained.

I can only imagine how I must have looked—a filthy, barefoot, four-year-old boy rummaging through garbage cans for something to eat. I don't know how long I'd been searching through the trash when a police officer on foot patrol discovered me. As he approached, I never thought to run. I suppose I wasn't afraid. When he asked me where I lived, I disobeyed my mother again and eagerly led him to our apartment. I knew she'd say I never should have let him in, but what was I supposed to do? I had tried as long as I could to keep it together while she was away, but I just couldn't any longer. We needed help.

If it had been a fairytale, the story would have ended here—just the way it does on television—with the little boy wearing the police officer's hat and eating an ice cream cone. That's not what happened. How was I to know I was getting my mother into trouble? There was no way for me to know that this event was the beginning of the rest of my life without her.

Once the officer was inside the apartment, it was painfully obvious that we had been left alone for more than a few hours. The apartment was filthy and in disarray, and all the food was gone. The police officer had no choice but to call the Bureau of Child Welfare.

When the car with the adults arrived to haul Keith and me away from our home, I cried and screamed at the top of my lungs, "I want Sherry! I want Sherry!"

I fought and screamed and cried with everything I had to stop them from taking us away. I have no recollection of being frightened while at home, even during the times my mother wasn't there. Leaving everything that was familiar, however, petrified me. Finally, I fell asleep in the car.

My next memory is of waking up in a new place. Its strangeness made me feel as if I were dreaming. Weird people—fat with bright red lipstick and a lot of makeup—were staring at me.

The strange new destination, it turns out, was the downtown location where kids were processed into foster care. After my initial intake interview, I underwent a series of evaluations, which included a medical exam to ensure that I had no communicable diseases. My biggest medical problem was severe tooth decay. Because of my mom's lack of prenatal care, I had been born with a calcium deficiency that led to a mouth full of rotten teeth and bad breath. Dental hygiene problems notwithstanding, Keith and I were deemed healthy enough to be placed in an emergency foster home that night.

Just hours after being snatched away from our mother's house, my brother and I arrived at the home of our first foster mother, Miss Fanny. Thanks to an attentive police officer and New York City's Bureau of Child Welfare, we had food, a place to sleep, and stability. You would think such comforts would have made me feel safe, but I did not feel safe at all. Going to my first foster home was traumatic, because I didn't want to be in an unfamiliar place with a bunch of strange people; I wanted to be with my mother in our house. I became confused and numb. I didn't understand what was happening; all my feelings of security vanished, and I became my only friend.

Miss Fanny lived in a New York brownstone, just as we had; but unlike my family, she owned hers, and the other occupants in the building were her tenants. She opened her door and ushered us in. I entered hesitantly and walked down the long corridor while the social worker placed Keith in her arms. The living room was bright and sunny and had a television. Delighted, I immediately ran to it and looked around to see what else was in the room.

Miss Fanny's house was crowded with a lot of interesting things that were off limits. I received my orders. "Don't touch this. Definitely don't touch that. And under no circumstances are you ever to touch those things," she said emphatically as she pointed to each object. It was overwhelming and impossible for a four-year-old. I wasn't used to so many things in one place, because my mom's place had been practically bare.

Miss Fanny's rules were simple: Don't touch; Sit down; Be quiet. But what four-year-old is able to do all that? I couldn't just sit still. I wanted to touch, examine, and play with things—especially the things that were forbidden. If I wasn't pulling and tangling the Scotch tape, I was emptying the salt-and-pepper shakers all over the floor. I was an active, little guy who was curious about everything. I wanted to talk and to be talked to. I liked talking—still do! My mother had talked to me all the time and answered my questions, but Miss Fanny didn't believe kids should make noise.

The old adage, "Kids should been seen and not heard," ranked right up there with her "Don't touch" rule. She kept telling me I talked too much and asked too many questions.

After a few slipups, I suffered the consequences—confinement in the crib that I shared with Keith. Because I was small for my age, the two of us comfortably slept together in our very own escape-proof cell. My most vivid memories of our stay with Miss Fanny are of being in the crib and watching a lot of television, which seemed to be on all the time. Television was fine, but why did we have to watch so much of it? I hardly ever went outside. Maybe Miss Fanny kept us in the crib all the time to keep me from running around and getting into trouble; I always seemed to be in trouble.

When Miss Fanny was present, I got along fine with her children, but as soon as she left the house, they stopped being nice to me. It was almost as if someone flipped a switch. Sometimes, they would team up and take turns hitting me for no reason at all. On other days, my fourteen-year-old foster sister would have me all to herself.

One day, she took me into a room, undressed me, and had me lay face up on the floor. She undressed too and gently laid her body on top of mine. She started moving and bouncing up and down on top of me. I don't know how long it lasted, and I didn't know exactly what she was doing, but I remember it made me feel confused and upset. I don't recall how many other encounters there were. Because I didn't know what she was doing or why she was doing it, I never told on her. What was there to tell? I remember my feelings and attitude changed after that, and I became more aggressive. Miss Fanny probably never imagined why I started acting so differently.

When I wasn't getting into trouble or being treated poorly by my foster brother and sister, I was wondering where my mother was and missing her terribly. It would be many years before I understood why she wasn't able to care for us.

It seems odd to me that I understood a lot about the circumstances that forced me to grow up quickly, but much of the foster care stuff baffled me for years. I knew that I didn't like living with strange people. I knew that I wanted to be with my real family. My memories of living at Miss Fanny's are like being enveloped in fog or a dark cloud. I kept hoping it would end and that I would wake up in my mother's arms again. I didn't feel as if I belonged there. I felt different from everybody around me and not in a good way. I couldn't express what I was feeling, nor did I realize that children who are separated from their birth parents usually have abandonment and trust issues. No one ever talked to me about what I felt, so I went on pretending I was okay and acting as if I didn't have questions about my family, particularly about my mom.

We stayed with Miss Fanny—and I endured the abuse from my foster brother and sister—for about a year while the authorities worked unsuccessfully to reunite us with our mother or to find relatives we could live with. Neither my mom's mother nor her siblings could care for us. Grandma was also a single mother and had five other children, several of them younger than my nineteen-year-old mom. Besides, as I later learned, Grandma didn't want us anyway. There was no effort to locate my father or anyone on his side of the family.

As for my mother, she continued to struggle with alcohol and drugs. It was a battle that cost her everything she had. With her children gone, there wasn't much for her to live for. As her pain grew deeper, there just weren't enough drugs to numb it. Whenever friends or family asked about her sons, and they asked often, she told them we were in Brooklyn with an aunt. That explanation was far better for her than to hear herself say, "I chose drugs over my kids, and the state took them."

One day, the social worker caught up with her; she was barely able to stand on her feet. She worked hard to pull it together long enough to have a reasonable conversation. The social worker was there on a mission to get Sherry to voluntarily relinquish her parental rights, so my brother and I could be adopted. But my mother just couldn't let us go. For the longest time, each visit from the social worker ended with the same response: "No." My mother was famous for her temper, so with each visit, the no became more animated, and the choice words before and after a bit harsher. On one of the last visits, my mother slapped the social worker for accusing her of being unfit to parent because she was an addict.

A few visits later, Sherry voluntarily relinquished her rights, finally admitting that her children deserved what she could not give them.

No one ever asked me what I wanted or even talked to me about it. I never even knew she had been found. Later, when I was nine or ten years old, my therapist, Dr. Lewis, explained all of this to me. I had always thought that my mom would never give us up and that maybe that was why we were foster children. When adoption became an option, my social workers starting revealing more to me.

But when I was five years old, no one told me anything. I wondered why my foster mom or my caseworker wouldn't talk to me about my family.

Even at age five, I knew enough to care about the decisions affecting my brother and me. But since no one was willing to explain anything to me or ask me how I felt about any of it, I quickly learned to do what was expected of me, and I kept all my memories, thoughts, and opinions locked inside my head. I didn't ask questions, and I smiled as if everything were okay.

Well, nothing in my life was okay. I could not think of anything but my mother and whether she was safe. I knew I was the "Little Man," but living in two worlds was rough; I was being forced to live in the present while I was clinging to the past.

♦ ♦ ♦

The day I was told we were going to long-term foster care, I recall being extremely afraid, even though I didn't understand what it meant. I remember watching *Speed Racer* and *Gigantor*, my favorite cartoons, and telling myself every few minutes, "It's going to be okay. Sherry's coming to get us. Yes, Sherry is coming to take us home. She *always* comes back. We're going to be okay." And when this rationale didn't work, I'd start singing some of my favorite songs to make me feel better—at least for a few minutes. I was particularly comforted by the Beatles' song, "Let It Be"and by Simon and Garfunkel's "Mrs. Robinson". I don't know why I developed such a mysterious attachment to those songs at so early an age; maybe they were my mother's favorites too. Even now, they continue to bring me a sense of comfort when I hear them.

I found no comfort, however, on the morning the officials came to Miss Fanny's door to take us to our long-term foster care home. Two very large adults filed in to take Keith and me away. They were there to help us, to take us to meet our new foster parents, but I was terrified. I screamed, scratched, bit, and cried hysterically. I held on to the walls, to the doors, to anything that I could to keep them from taking me.

While watching the movie, *Losing Isaiah* recently, I was reminded of that day. It took me right back to the day we left Miss Fanny's, and for just one moment, I was five again, experiencing the pain and anguish of being taken from one home to another. And just like Isaiah, I was defenseless. I could do nothing to stop them from taking us away. I hoped they would allow us to stay—not so much because I liked living at Miss Fanny's but more because I didn't want to be taken to another strange place where I'd meet new strange people.

They eventually managed to put me in the car alongside Keith, where I promptly fell asleep, exhausted.

After a short drive to the Catholic Home Bureau, I was awakened and introduced to a dark-complexioned woman with pearly white teeth. She was wearing a red coat with a matching pillbox hat. Her husband, a tall man with a very light complexion and a receding hairline, looked distinguished as he stood beside her with his navy blazer and gray slacks. I could not help noticing that he had perfect teeth too. They didn't dress like anyone I'd ever met before.

After formal introductions, I was told that my brother and I were going to be living with them from then on.

Chapter 2
WHAT ABOUT THE CHILDREN?

So what about the children—remember when we were children
And if not for those who loved us and who cared
enough to show us, where would we be today?
—Yolanda Adams

Doris Maxine Jenkins and Robert Louis Jenkins were my new foster parents. They told me that they had a son—Robert Jr., called Robbie—whom we would meet later. He was about three years older than I was, and I was so excited about getting another brother.

They seemed eager to have us join their family, perhaps because my foster father had grown up in an orphanage. Later on, as our relationship grew, he often spoke about his experiences as an orphan during the Depression. He recounted how he had closed his eyes one morning to say grace, and when he had opened them, his oatmeal had been gone. After that had happened a few times, he had started saying grace with his finger firmly in the center of his breakfast. That act had stopped future breakfast thefts. The story was funny the way he told it, but the visual image made the thought of being in an orphanage unbearable to me. He had promised himself that one day he would give a child the home he had always wanted as a little boy. As the months turned into years with the Jenkins family, I was grateful that he'd kept that promise, but I had a hard time adjusting to a new set of parents, a new older brother, and a new set of rules.

When we met at the Catholic Home Bureau, the first few minutes were spent getting acquainted, before Keith and I were led to the Jenkins's family car—a very sharp red and white Oldsmobile with wings on the back. As Keith and I huddled up next to each other in the backseat, I began to feel overwhelmed by everything. The car seemed so big, and I felt so small. I was leaving Miss Fanny and going to live with people we had only just met. I had no idea what awaited us at the Jenkins's house. It was a lot for a five-year-old to process.

As we made our way to our new home in Crown Heights, Brooklyn, I remember Mr. Jenkins looking in the rearview mirror at me.

"What do you want to call us?"

Without hesitation, I said, "Mom and Dad."

It would be the first time I had ever called anybody Mom and Dad, and from that moment on, that's who they were for Keith and me.

When we arrived at our new home, I cautiously scoped out the environment. The apartment was nothing like any home I had ever seen. It was clean and orderly. The living room had plush, rust-colored carpet, and plastic slipcovers were on the furniture. I had to ask what the big, brown, wooden thing against the wall was; I'd never seen a piano before. After Dad told me, he said that Robbie took piano lessons and that maybe I might someday too. I had no clue what piano lessons were. The bedroom Keith and I shared with Robbie was light green, brightly lit, and very neat. Everything seemed to have its proper place. I remember thinking, *Boy, oh boy, these people have so many nice things.* I wasn't used to all that nice stuff. It was even better than Miss Fanny's place, because it was neat and spacious, there was a piano, and all the furniture matched. Then I started to feel scared and could not keep still or get comfortable. All I could do was worry whether the big men would come back to take us away.

Our health was poor when we arrived at the Jenkins's. Our calcium was so deficient—exacerbated by the fact that my birth mother had hated milk—that two-year-old Keith was still unable to walk because his bones were so fragile. On one of our frequent visits to the pediatrician, Mom Jenkins was told that being carried too frequently was as much to blame for my baby brother's fragile bones as the calcium deficiency. People picked Keith up constantly, because he was such an incredibly handsome little boy. No one seemed to realize that being held so much discouraged him from walking.

Mom Jenkins also took me to a dentist, who determined that my rotten teeth would have to be extracted to give the permanent teeth a chance to grow in correctly. By the time I turned six, I had had nine teeth extracted and hideous silver caps placed on the teeth that remained. I thought that the caps made me look ugly, and they added to my growing sense of feeling different. In an effort to fit in, I would take a safety pin and try to pry them off when no one was looking. One day, I finally succeeded. I ran to Mom Jenkins screaming, "Mom! Mom! Mom! My cap fell off," hoping that she would let me leave it off for good. Instead, she promptly took me to the dentist to have it replaced.

◆　◆　◆

Robbie, Keith, and I shared a room—they shared the top and bottom of a bunk-bed, and I had my own folding ottoman. I wanted to share the high-riser, too, and I didn't know why I'd been given my own bed. Was it because I was a bed wetter or because I didn't seem to enjoy being around other kids? I was self-conscious and insecure, and I desperately wanted to fit in. To make matters worse, my new foster brother, Robbie, was brilliant, was always well behaved, and excelled in school. Much to my dismay, he and Keith instantly bonded and became very close. It didn't take long before I began to resent both of them.

"Robbie is so smart," everyone would say.

"Isn't Keith cute? Just look at those big eyes," others would gush.

People never had much to say about me. My breath always stank because of my rotting teeth, and I had those awful silver caps. My behavior was not the best either. Sandwiched between Robbie and Keith, I was lost. I didn't fit in, and no one seemed to notice me. Eventually, I figured out that people paid attention to me when I was in trouble, so I gave them trouble—a lot of it.

I started stealing and lying shortly after I arrived at the Jenkins's home. The living room was one of my favorite places to hit. Despite having been told on numerous occasions that it was off limits unless an adult was present, I ventured in to take whatever was of real interest to me, especially money. Dad Jenkins used to keep excess change hidden on the top shelf of the bookcase. I remember the rush I would get from taking things that belonged to someone else. The real thrill was in knowing that I usually wasn't caught. Even when I was, the attention I received, however negative, was better than no attention at all.

In addition to thieving, I found myself making up elaborate stories, hoping that people would be impressed and listen to me. I really wanted to be heard and noticed. I was so mixed up inside, in so much pain, and so confused that I was willing to do whatever it took to get attention, even if it meant lying.

Mom Jenkins really seemed to like my stories at first. Eventually, however, she and almost everyone else caught on, and no one would believe anything I said. I was branded a liar and a thief—tags that would follow me throughout school.

I started first grade just before my sixth birthday, which was a considerable accomplishment given all the drama in my life. At St. Francis of Assisi on Lincoln Road in Brooklyn, all eyes seemed to focus on my metallic teeth. To add to my allure, I started wearing glasses. Even I couldn't deny that I looked like a little geek, and my classmates teased me mercilessly. Recess was open season, and I became the butt of many jokesters' pranks.

I didn't like myself at all. I was confused and overwhelmed by all the things that were happening in my life. Interacting with kids who lived with their real parents and shared the same last names got to me from time to time. They all seemed so happy, so perfect. They certainly didn't get into trouble the way I did.

As for my schoolwork, I always hoped the tests would be multiple choice, so I wouldn't have to read the question and could randomly select a, b, or c. It wasn't that I was lazy; I just couldn't concentrate long enough to read an entire question. Sometimes my multiple-choice method worked, and I got good grades; sometimes I got glaring Ds or Fs, causing my low self-esteem to plummet even further.

To escape, I did what many children in distress do: I daydreamed a lot. I'd drift away and think about my real family: *What are they doing? What do they look like? Do I look like them? Am I that ugly? Why don't they want me? Where is my mother? I wish I could be good; maybe then, people would like me, and maybe I would fit in.* These thoughts consumed me and kept me from being a good student.

I found the rigidity and complexity of Catholic school difficult. There were just too many rules, so I tested as many of them as possible to see how much I could get away with. In short order, I became the class clown. The nuns definitely needed some humor in their lives, and who better to entertain them than attention-starved Shane?

I thrived on rattling their cages. I wonder if I'm the only one who ever imagined pulling the habit off a nun's head. Because of my constant misbehavior, I lived in the principal's office. Sometimes my teacher, Sister Collette, would punish me by making me sit in a trashcan with my legs hanging out. Then she'd add insult to injury by letting other students empty the shavings from their pencil sharpeners on me.

If I wasn't lying or clowning at school, I was stealing. My parents would give me money to buy books, but I would spend it instead. When I was short on cash, I stole money from my classmates' book bags. Money my parents gave me for my student savings account never made it to the bank, because I spent that too.

I thought I was putting it over on everybody, but by the time I got to fourth grade, my reputation as a liar and thief was solidified. I also became known as the kid who couldn't pay attention. At every parent-teacher conference, I overheard my teachers tell Mom Jenkins that I was "not working up to my full potential." That one statement meant extra punishment for not behaving correctly in school. I spent many recesses, timeouts, and afternoons after school standing in the corner facing a wall, angry, confused, or drifting in a daydream. My reputation as "the worst kid in the classroom" gradually changed to being one of the worst kids in the school.

By the time I entered the fifth grade, all the teachers knew that whoever got Shane as a student was in for a challenge, and they treated me accordingly. Sister Miriam Anita, the meanest nun of them all, constantly threatened to have me transferred to public school if I continued to misbehave. Public school was the worst possible punishment that could happen to a kid. The nuns were quick to remind anyone who stepped out of line that public school kids were mean and that kids who went to public school got beaten up *all the time.* Public school sounded a lot like Catholic school with me as a lead character, but whenever I heard "the threat," I'd straighten up. I have Sister Miriam Anita to thank for my sporadic good behavior, but even under the threat of expulsion, I would revert to acting out—and not just at school.

My lack of concentration led school administrators to evaluate me for special education classes. No one realized the problem was simply what's commonly known now as attention deficit disorder (ADD). There was little known about ADD then. Fortunately, I was never placed in the special education program, but my struggle to focus on schoolwork and to concentrate continued. As much as I tried to calm my mind and still my body, I couldn't. I knew there was something different about me. Why couldn't I act and think like the other children? Why was I always in trouble?

My disruptive, impulsive, and outright aggressive behavior was never associated with a neurological condition that caused my brain to function differently from others. Had diagnostic tools and resources for ADD kids been available to me then, my early educational experience could have been very different. I would have been taught how to adapt to the way my brain functioned instead of being pressured to change what couldn't be changed. My teachers would have shown me ways to overcome my learning difficulties and leverage my strengths, making me a more confident child and a better student. The best part is that I would not have grown up thinking I wasn't good at academics.

The problem was that my brain processed information so rapidly that, while people were talking, I had already gone on to something else. In math, for instance, I would often figure out the problem in my head and stop focusing on the remainder of the lesson. When called upon, I frequently gave the correct answer, but I got in trouble when I could not adequately explain the steps I took to arrive at my calculation. The "process thing" just didn't work for me. I'd bypass one or more steps and race through the equation. I figured, *Why go to all that trouble if there is a quicker solution?* Well, as I would eventually learn, quick solutions do not work for everything in life.

◆　◆　◆

During those initial years with the Jenkins family, we would sometimes visit Mr. Jenkins's younger sister, whom we called Aunt Flip. Unlike her older brother, Aunt Flip had very straight hair and looked like a white woman—two traits that were an immense source of pride for her. She would tell me that the "whiter" I looked and behaved, the more successful I would be in life. She made me pinch my nose so that it wouldn't be so wide. That way, with my "fair" complexion, she thought I could pass for white. Well, my nose is still wide, and my skin hasn't lightened over the years, so I guess I won't be passing for white after all. Sorry to disappoint you, Aunt Flip.

One day while Aunt Flip was babysitting Keith and me at her house, I found some matches and snuck into the downstairs bathroom to play with them. I struck a few of them, tossing them in the toilet bowl to extinguish their tiny flames. Intrigued, I set the toilet paper on fire, which very quickly got out of control. Panicked, I threw the roll into the toilet, and a huge cloud of smoke billowed out. I ran upstairs yelling and screaming with every ounce of conviction I could muster that my "doo-doo" was on fire, hoping Aunt Flip would actually believe that poop was a highly combustible substance (I never said I was a good liar).

When I went home that evening, I got my butt torn up. I knew enough to know that foster parents are not supposed to spank children, but the Jenkins treated me as their own. That night, Mr. Jenkins gave me a beating I will never forget. He said he was beating me out of love and that I would remember that day as long as I lived. Well, he was right. I never forgot how, with every lash of the belt, Mr. Jenkins kept telling me why he was beating me and how much he loved me. From that day forward, I never played with matches again.

My relationship with Dad Jenkins was different from Keith's and Robbie's. He had a ferocious temper, and I was afraid of him, just as everyone else in the house was. As tough as he was, I really did feel he loved me. He seemed to enjoy spending time with me and talking to me, and we liked to do many of the same things (such as watching *60 Minutes* with Mike Wallace). Dad enjoyed teaching me to fix things around the house as much as I enjoyed learning from him. I liked his company and behaved differently when he was around—a fact that didn't go unnoticed by Mom Jenkins. She would often remind me of this split in my personality when I was acting out during his absence.

I believe he was the only person in the house who really understood me.

In retrospect, I think I was his favorite, in spite of the fact that I was a bad kid. He saw my potential and understood my pain. He'd been abandoned at birth too and had made his way through life without love, support, or nurturing parents. Perhaps he saw a bit of himself in me.

♦ ♦ ♦

My jealously of Robbie and Keith continued to grow throughout elementary school. They were so perfect. Even when they misbehaved, things just seemed to turn out better for them. Keith, the cute one and the youngest, floated on a stream of constant compliments and attention. He was smart too, and I hated that.

One day, we were running through the house and I knew Keith was a few feet behind me, so I intentionally slammed a door shut. He crashed into the door so hard that he was knocked unconscious. I was scared when I saw my brother stretched out on the floor. His big lips turned blue, and Mom Jenkins had to use smelling salts to bring him around. Then she knocked the living daylights out of me, and I deserved it.

As if having a real mother and father weren't enough of a reason to resent Robbie, he also turned out to be a child prodigy. He spoke three different languages and played six musical instruments. Unbelievable! I spent many an evening at Carnegie Hall listening to Robbie's musical recitals.

Ultimately, my resentment toward Robbie grew to the point of violence. One day, without provocation, I punched him in the stomach as hard as I could. I knew he was soft and would not fight back, so I wasn't surprised when he went crying to Mom. Her response was, "If you won't defend yourself, you deserved it."

That statement may have been a good lesson in self-defense for Robbie but not for an angry, jealous brother. From that day forward, I ruled both my older foster brother and my younger brother, but my satisfaction was fleeting.

Stuck between adorable Keith and Robbie the genius, shameless Shane was in a difficult situation. The older I got, the worse I felt about myself. I frowned a lot and avoided smiling because of those silver-capped teeth and because Mom Jenkins often told me I smiled like a monkey. Then there were the glasses. Aunt Flip said they made me look like an owl. The other kids thought the glasses had more of a Poindexter mystique and teased me every chance they got.

I could not stop wetting the bed no matter how hard I tried, and I was so ashamed. No one liked me; no one understood me; I didn't fit in anywhere; and my caregivers thought I was a monkey-grinning, owl-faced, bed-wetting liar and thief—not a great self-image for anyone, especially a child desperately in need of love.

As if I wasn't confused enough, puberty kicked in, and Paulette caught my eye. At age thirteen, she was choc-o-late with kinky, rough hair, and I liked it. Paulette lived down the street, and sometimes, we'd play house in the stairwell of the six-story building where I lived. That's where she taught me "the nasty." I had no idea my body could feel and do the things it did on the roof that day. It felt good, but I didn't understand what had happened. The excitement of having sex was scary at first.

Pleasure won out over fear, because soon after my first encounter with Paulette, I tried several times to make myself feel and do those things again. How Mom Jenkins figured out what I was up to in the privacy of the locked bathroom, I'll never know, but one day I overheard her asking Robbie what he thought she should do about my self-discovery.

"Leave him alone. It's normal," Robbie answered.

So against her better judgment, she overlooked my indiscretions and never talked to me about them.

As close as I felt to Dad Jenkins, I was uncomfortable talking to him about sex, and going to stern Mom Jenkins was definitely out of the question. While walking home from school, I eventually detoured to the neighborhood library in search of books on human sexuality to help me understand what I was experiencing.

Paulette and I continued our secret rooftop rendezvous, which I never told anyone about. What would they think if they knew I was "doing it" and having all these strange new feelings on top of my behavior problems?

Months later at a children's Halloween party, I had a different kind of sexual encounter with the host of the party, a white man who lived across the street from us. Midway through the party, he led me to his basement. I remember wondering where everyone was and how I had wound up down there alone with the fat, greasy-looking, white man. Then he started touching me all over. I started to run around the chairs, which were scattered about from playing games. I ran up the steps, and the door was locked. He called after me. I don't remember exactly what he said, but it was something along the lines of "Big boys don't run." Then he unlocked the door, and I ran home.

Another time, while I was playing in front of my building, the same man offered me potato chips if I'd let him touch me again. I liked chips, but I did not get in the car. Just looking at him made me sick. I later learned he had molested another child in the neighborhood. Even though I never told Mom and Dad Jenkins about the incidents, I was fortunate to have an adult in my life in whom I felt comfortable confiding—Dr. Lewis, a therapist whom I had started with when I was nine. Dr. Lewis and I talked a lot about my loneliness and my dreams of having my own family. She knew I never felt like I fit in anywhere, because I was always in trouble for something with my attention deficit disorder and my acting out.

Mom Jenkins was providing me with all of the right things a child should have, but she wasn't very affirming or nurturing. Much later in life, I came to understand the family dynamics that were at play, which had very little to do with me. I reminded her of Mr. Jenkins, and because he identified so much with me as an orphan himself and as the only other light-complexioned family member and one who was filled with curiosity, we could relate to one another. I was affectionately called his "number two son." I think I paid a price for this when he wasn't around, which was most of the time. I don't remember Mom Jenkins ever hugging me or asking me how things were.

I couldn't have ever told her about the attempted abuse I suffered. So Dr. Lewis and I talked about these kinds of things. She would often tell me that I was special and smart and that my dreams could come true.

When I told her about the incidents with the man, she listened and reassured me that it was not my fault and that I had done nothing wrong. It wasn't until I became an advocate for children that I learned the alarming statistics on child molestation. One out of every four girls and one out of every five boys are molested before reaching the age of eighteen.

◆　◆　◆

Like most kids my age, I wanted to have my own pocket money, and I was lucky enough to get a paper route. The pay was good, and the tips were great. I'd been on the job for a few weeks when, one day on one of my regular stops, I rang the front doorbell, and no one answered. I turned the knob, and the door opened. A pair of pants was hanging over a chair, and I couldn't resist pushing the door all the way open, sneaking inside, and going through the pockets. I left the newspaper (as evidence, of course) and raced out of the apartment. I don't remember how much money I got, but I felt rich. It was like Christmas in July. I went down the street to the store and bought a tape recorder and a bunch of other things.

When I got home and Mom Jenkins saw my new purchases, she

correctly deduced that I had stolen the money and was convinced I had taken it from her purse. Dad Jenkins also thought that I had stolen the money but from his stash in the living room. *What hypocrites*, I thought. Here they were chastising me for stealing, and both of them were trying to claim something that did not belong to either of them. I listened in silence as my accusers argued over whose money had been lifted. If they knew where I had really gotten it from, it would have made the situation worse, so I never said a word.

Confused, distressed, and plagued by trouble, I concluded that the best solution for my problems was to run away. The next Sunday morning, I took all of my paper route tips and my newly acquired loot, hooked up with my friend Stacey who lived downstairs, and took off. We thought we were set, but the money ran out after our first stop at White Castle for hamburgers and fries. He'd barely licked the grease from his lips when he punked out and went back home. I didn't want to go back home, but I did. Less than two hours on the road and I was back. No one even knew I was AWOL.

I gradually grew so unhappy there that I felt as if I couldn't do anything right and that no one liked me. Even Dad Jenkins's patience was wearing thin. I was eleven years old and had been seeing a therapist for two years, but therapy didn't help me improve my self-image. It made me feel even more different from my brothers and classmates. As my self-esteem fell, my behavior worsened. I told Dr. Lewis about my loneliness and the deep hole that losing my mother had left in my heart. That pain was still strong, even though I thought less and less about seeing her again as time went on.

My arrival at the Jenkins home had triggered daydreams of adoption and of sharing their surname. I thought that change might fill the emptiness inside me. For some reason, the thought of signing my name "Shane Jenkins" was the most appealing part of it. I wanted to belong to someone, to fit in. If I had the same name as the family I lived with, people wouldn't be able to tell from my name that I was different.

My therapist told me that adoption was permanent, and if Mom and Dad Jenkins adopted us, Keith and I would be secure forever. No more sudden moves, no more strange people. In one of my therapy sessions, I wrote a three-page play called *The Adopted Child* in which the Jenkins family adopted me. In the end, that's all it was—a play.

Keith and I lived in the Jenkins home for more than seven years, and we were given the best of everything. We were nurtured, disciplined, and humbled, and were given a lot of love. Never did they treat us any differently from their birth son. We even dressed in matching clothing, as if we were triplets. We went to the same private schools, got the same medical care, and shared the same room.

Nevertheless, I always knew I was different. I didn't talk about it, but I knew my name was Salter and theirs was Jenkins. Every time I had to write my name on a school paper or went to the doctor and she called me by my last name, I was reminded that I didn't really belong.

During our seventh year with the Jenkins family, Mr. Pointer, my social worker, told me that my brother and I would be moving from our long-term foster care placement to an adoptive home soon.

I don't remember anyone explaining to us why we couldn't be adopted by the Jenkinses. I didn't ask. I just assumed that I was too much trouble. I wasn't in a good place—no matter how hard I tried to pretend. Why didn't I think it was okay under the circumstances to be confused, hurt, and angry? Quietly to myself and alone in my mind, I retaliated.

So what if they don't want me? I'm going to get my own family anyway. Maybe my new family will even think I'm cute. I hope I can stop being so much trouble; maybe then they'll love me forever.

But my first question upon hearing the news was, *"Will my name be the same as my new parents'?"*

"Yes, Shane," Mr. Pointer said.

I was ecstatic.

Due to our advanced ages, Keith and I were classified as "hard to place." In most states, children aged eighteen months and older are deemed hard to place, because babies are considered more desirable, adapt better, and exhibit fewer abandonment issues. Also, we were black and came as a package, our chances of getting a good permanent home decreased further.

For a fleeting moment, I wished I didn't have a brother. Maybe then my chances would be better. Maybe people wouldn't compare me to him and talk about how cute he was all the time. However, in reality, my brother was my world. We were joined at the hip. I wouldn't go anywhere without him or ever leave him behind.

The recruitment process to find the best adoptive family moved very quickly after our photographs appeared in the *Amsterdam News*. I barely recognized the description of myself, even with the fictitious name:

Aside from being a very handsome-looking, bright, and creative young man, Sean loves singing and dancing and writing plays. He has a warm, outgoing personality and a good wit and is delightful company. He also makes friends easily once he gets to know you and has very little difficulty in relating to friendly adults. That's because he says, "I like people."

When "advertising" for adoptive families, it is common practice for agencies to give children fictitious names for privacy, but somehow Keith's real name made it into print.

Several families responded to the newspaper article, and eventually the most suitable family was selected. Eager to have a permanent home, I was determined to be on my best behavior. If I could be perfect, someone would finally want me and love me. I got the feeling that our new parents wanted me to be perfect too.

During the preplacement weekend visits, there always seemed to be much excitement over our impending arrival. We were given everything we wanted. There seemed to be no limit to our new parents' generosity and kindness. A steady stream of relatives came by the house to meet us, or we drove to their homes to meet our prospective new grandparents, aunts, uncles, and cousins. We were introduced as the latest addition to the family, and it was great getting all of the attention and repeatedly hearing how handsome both Keith and I were. A few relatives even commented on "the strong family resemblance."

On one particular visit when Mr. Pointer, our social worker, dropped us off, he asked our soon-to-be parents when they would bring us back. Our new dad's response was "the twelfth of never." I thought, *How's that for having a real home and family? Our names will be the same as theirs. My dream is coming true. I will have a real family of my own, a place where I belong.* We finally had it made.

With "the twelfth of never" still ringing in my ears, I went back to the Jenkins's home confident and obnoxious in the belief that my turn had finally come. Not only was I going to be moving in with a new family, but they were also rich. I was moving up in the world, going from an apartment in Crown Heights, Brooklyn, to a townhouse duplex in Co-Op City in the Bronx.

Nonetheless, I was angry with Mom and Dad Jenkins for not adopting us. They had never discussed their reasons with us, and we had never asked. Because no one had told me why my foster parents wouldn't adopt me, I told myself that I would show them that their rejection didn't matter to me. I danced around the house, making up songs with words intended to hurt my foster family: "I'm so glad I'm leaving, because I'm going to a new home where people will love me forever." With each verse, I kept getting louder and louder to be sure that everybody in the house heard me clearly; that way they wouldn't know that deep inside I felt rejected, scared, and lonely.

Once the paperwork was finalized, I really started acting out. A part of me really didn't want to leave what was familiar and safe. I didn't want to start all over again with another set of parents, a new set of rules, a new school, and a new set of friends. I wasn't sure how well I'd adapt.

Then there was part of me that looked forward to the new beginning, the chance to start all over again. I hoped the new people would understand me. I wanted to try, but I wasn't sure I could hold up my end of the bargain. Also, adoption was a new option for us, and I didn't know the rules of the game.

I don't know if the Jenkins family ever knew how conflicted I was, because I went out of my way to act as if I were happy to be leaving, but my act was short-lived and probably about as convincing as one of my most transparent lies.

A few short weeks of boastful indifference and feigned happiness abruptly ended the day Keith and I left the Jenkins home for good. We were finally being adopted. It should have been the happiest day of my life, but I cried and cried and cried.

"Mom, I don't want to go," I sobbed, hugging her as tight as I could. "Please, Mom, please."

My foster brother Robbie started crying, too. I didn't think he even liked me. Why was he crying? *He gets to have his parents all to himself,* I thought. But when he hugged me and said good bye, I knew it was real.

I looked up at Mom and Dad, and they were crying, too. Why? I had thought that they wanted us to go.

Mom Jenkins never showed much affection, but at that moment, she held me and said, "You'll be okay, son."

She tried her best to put a positive face on things. "You've got a new family waiting for you and Keith. Be good," she said, "and remember, we love you. The Roberts will take good care of you and Keith. You wait and see. You'll forget all about us after a while."

"No, Mommy," I wailed. "I'll never forget you. I promise."

We hugged, and I continued to cry uncontrollably.

"Don't let me go," I pleaded.

She just pushed me away.

"It's time, son," Dad Jenkins said.

"No. No!" I screamed.

I grabbed Keith, and the waiting adults grabbed me.

My instinct was to fight as hard as I could to stop them from taking me away. But suddenly, I surrendered. I didn't scream, scratch, kick, or bite. I took Keith by the hand and let them lead us outside to the waiting car. As we drove away, I wiped my eyes and thought about my new life and how wonderful the new family was going to be.

Chapter 3
GOD BLESS THE DREAMER

Put some love in your heart, put some heart in your love,
And don't let the doubt steer you wrong.
There'll be something out of nothing,
When love comes along.
—Tamyra Gray

When we arrived at our new adoptive home, the Roberts were excited to see us. Mr. Roberts worked for the Port Authority as a bus driver, and Mrs. Roberts was a photographer and a beautician. She was a fox. They had one son named Anthony. Anthony had seen our pictures in the *Amsterdam News* and begged his parents to let him have two brothers. On our absolute best behavior, we tried to behave like two model foster children. Everything in the article seemed to be as stated. Keith and I were okay kids. Things were going really well. But a month after our arrival, the honeymoon ended.

During the preplacement visits, Anthony and I had gotten along great, but as soon as Keith and I moved in, he became resentful. I guess he thought having brothers would be a lot more fun than being an only child, but he soon learned that having two brothers meant sharing space, food, and his parents' attention. We would fight a lot about seconds at the dinner table. I think he was all right with sharing attention and living space, but he was big, and his eating less was out of the question.

We would also fight over the pettiest nonsense whenever Mr. and Mrs. Roberts weren't home. We would chase each other through the house with the rage of mortal enemies determined to fight to the death. I was usually the one who picked up a stick. I wanted to beat him upside his head every chance I could get. I never could though. Anthony was no Robbie. He was a football player, and he could fight. I wasn't used to that. He would wrestle me down or body-slam me once he caught me.

When I lost a fight to Anthony—and I usually did—I would run to the closest pay phone and call Mom Jenkins to complain and cry. I would tell her that I missed all of them and wanted to come back home.

Without fail and with incredible clarity, Mom Jenkins would painfully remind me that the Roberts were my family and that Keith and I could never come back to live with her, Robbie, and Dad Jenkins.

"You got to make this work, Shane," she would say.

"But I'd rather live with you."

"You have a permanent home and a family that will adopt you. You have a new life now," she would remind me.

I'd hang up disappointed but motivated to try to get along with Anthony and stay out of trouble.

There were things that I liked about the Roberts. They were much younger than Mom and Dad Jenkins, and their house was bigger. Because Mrs. Roberts was a photographer, I took an interest in photography, and they bought me my first camera. All my friends thought my new mom was cool too.

It didn't take long before I started making friends in my new neighborhood.

I really hit it off with Todd, a tall, smooth-talking guy with curly hair. All the girls were crazy about him. I thought Todd's single mom was so cool, because she would often go out on dates, giving Todd and me a chance to get into all kinds of mischief.

One of my favorite neighborhood friends was a gorgeous Jamaican girl named Carmen. We would exchange notes and an occasional kiss when we passed one another in the hallways of the apartment building. One day, I got her to agree to skip school and go home with me. We got to the house, went to my room, got out of our clothes, and started to have sex. Just as things were steaming up, my foster mom came home and caught us. She screamed and told us to put our clothes on. That's when my real trouble began.

Of course, Mrs. Roberts told Mr. Roberts what I had done.

"Shane, I'm extremely disappointed in you. Not only have you tarnished the reputation of this family, but also, you have compromised the reputation of that girl and her family. I won't tolerate that kind of behavior in my house again. Do you hear me? I'm beginning to believe you can't be trusted to do what's expected of you." He was furious.

Although I pleaded with her not to, Mrs. Roberts telephoned Carmen's parents and told them what we had done. Carmen's parents punished her by beating her terribly with an extension cord and forbidding her from ever speaking to me again.

After I told Todd about the incident, it didn't take long for the news to spread. Everyone at school was talking about the fact that we were caught, which, ironically, made me more popular. I was now running neck and neck with Todd for the title of coolest dude in school, because everyone knew I was getting my groove on with the girls.

About a week or so of being in the doghouse at home and having every privilege taken away started to make me feel like I wasn't good enough to be a member of the family. My lying, stealing, and bed-wetting increased. Then one day my whole world came to a screeching halt.

Keith and I had been living with our new family for only about two months when my social worker, Mr. Pointer, unexpectedly made a visit to my school. I was called out of homeroom and told to report to the main office. As soon as I entered, my heart stopped. Mr. Pointer was standing at the counter waiting with a sad look on his face.

"We need to talk, Shane," he said as he led me back into the hallway. "The Roberts called."

I immediately thought, *Oh, oh.* I knew enough to know that his referring to them as "the Roberts" instead of "your parents" was a bad omen.

"Things are not working out as they had hoped," he went on to say. "They want you and Keith to leave."

I couldn't believe it.

I struggled to get words out.

"How long before we have to leave?"

With no detectable show of emotion, he said, "Tomorrow."

I was struck by lightning, and my fragile heart was fried. It didn't seem to matter that I would turn thirteen in a few days or that we had made plans to celebrate Thanksgiving as a family. In fact, no one seemed to mention it. I was crumbling but couldn't move. All the hope and trust I had placed in so many adults—adults who kept letting me go, passing me off—died as I leaned against the wall in that hallway.

Sherry, Miss Fanny, Mom and Dad Jenkins, a host of nameless adults working in the foster care system, my teachers, the nuns—none of them could save me from yet another set of parents who were sending us back. It felt as if we were cargo with a stamp that said "Return to Sender." I would never trust again, and I would never believe the words "I love you."

"Mr. Pointer, why? Why don't they want me? Do adults ever mean what they say?" I asked while fighting back the tears as a new sense of rage welled up inside me. "I thought they meant it when they said 'the twelfth of never.' Even the shrink said adoption was permanent; so what happened? What did I do that was so terrible?"

Mr. Pointer tried to console me as best he could.

"Shane, you and Keith will be okay," he said.

"Okay, Mr. Pointer? Okay?" I repeated, my voice rising. "What did I do that was so terrible? Tell me what I did! Where am I going to go?"

He quietly and calmly explained that Keith and I would be going to an emergency foster home in the South Bronx. We were going to be moving from the somewhat upscale Co-Op City to a housing project in the area where I was born. I knew it would be rough.

"Couldn't you find any place better than that?" I complained.

I went numb. I retreated into a dark blanket of fog and confusion. They killed the spirit of that little boy who so desperately wanted love and acceptance. My childhood innocence was snatched away forever during that ten-minute conversation with Mr. Pointer.

I told Mr. Pointer I needed to say good-bye to my friend before I left, because that would be my last day at the school. I couldn't leave without saying good-bye to Todd. I found him after school, hanging out in the park and told him I was moving away the next day. He was shocked when I told him that I was a foster child and that the Roberts were not my real parents.

"My name really isn't Shane Roberts. It's Shane Salter."

"Man, stop lying. Why are you messing with me like that?" he said. When he realized I wasn't kidding, I could see real sadness in his face. Then he asked me where I was going.

"I don't really know, Todd. They tell me it's a family in the South Bronx," I said, as tears began to roll down my cheeks.

Todd tried his best to console me.

"Don't cry, Shane. We'll stay in touch. You'll still be living in the Bronx."

"Maybe I can come visit sometimes," I said.

My next task was to tell my brother Keith that we were going to have to leave yet another home. Just like me, I knew he really wanted this adoption to work. How could I break his heart by telling him that the Roberts wanted us to leave? I found him in our bedroom listening to Natalie Cole's, "Good Morning Heartache." How ironic.

"Hey, Keith," I said. "I need to talk to you. It's important. I'm sorry, but we have to leave the Roberts. Mr. Pointer is coming to get us tomorrow."

"Why? They don't want us anymore?" He looked as sad and confused as I had only hours earlier.

"Don't worry little brother; we're going to be okay."

I didn't have a clue what "being okay" really meant. Because the adults around me always said that whenever I was moving to another home, that's what I told Keith. He didn't know what "being okay" meant either.

That night as we started to pack, I heard my soon-to-be-ex dad come in the house. A few minutes later, I went into his room to beg him not to send us back. Nothing I said seemed to change his mind.

"Shane, you created this situation. It's your fault that things didn't work out. You and Keith have disrupted this family long enough. It's time for you to leave. This has been a difficult time for us. I almost lost my wife once," he went on to say, "and I'm not going to let anyone or anything come between us again."

I fell to my knees crying and begging, "Please, Dad, don't send us back."

"Shane, it's too late. The decision has been made. Now go back to your room and finish packing."

Through the heartbreak, I mustered up the strength to tell myself that I could handle whatever situation we might have to deal with in our emergency foster home. I was twelve, but what about Keith? I was very worried about him. He understood far less than I did. Now that I was back to being his parent again, I needed to find a way to comfort him, to reassure him, but all I could do was apologize.

"I'm sorry, Keith. I'm so sorry."

We finished our packing and went to bed, thinking that m aybe they would change their minds by the next day.

When I awoke the next morning, my head seemed cloudy, and I was overwhelmed by an incredible isolation. I felt like the unwanted, motherless child that I was.

Of course, the Roberts had not changed their minds, and Mr. Pointer did not pick us up. Our ex-parents placed our belongings and us in the car and drove very quickly to the agency. During the entire ride, they kept saying the same thing over and over: "You blew it, Shane. You blew a perfectly good home and family who loved you."

Under my breath I mumbled, "If you really love us, why are you giving us back?"

"As long as you continue lying, stealing, and wetting the bed, you will never have a good home," Mr. Roberts declared.

That car ride and their loud voices will be forever etched in my mind. I couldn't see or hear anything else. It was like a bad dream. To make matters worse, when we pulled up in front of the foster care agency at 1011 First Avenue, the Roberts pulled us from the car, dumped us on the curb, and sped away. Keith and I were left standing all alone with our clothes in garbage bags. We looked at each other for a minute, and then I took Keith's hand and walked with him into the lobby of the huge, forty-story office building.

I told the security guard seated in the lobby at the front desk who we were and what had just happened. He went back outside with us to retrieve our clothes, and after asking us which agency we belonged to, he called someone from the Catholic Home Bureau, and we were escorted upstairs. Right away, we were told about the next family we would be living with, headed by a Mr. and Mrs. Balfour.

While we waited to be taken to the Balfour home, I made a decision not to steal from people anymore. As I saw it, the new foster home was another chance for a new beginning. No one had to know anything about my past unless I told them about it or showed them. I didn't want to be known as a liar and a thief anymore. I didn't want people hiding their purses and wallets and talking about me behind my back. I couldn't handle that baggage anymore, not with everything else. I was no longer going to let my bad behavior prevent me from getting ahead. If it was going to stop me from getting a home, I wanted it gone. As of that day, anything that was going to stop me from reaching my dreams was *gone*—whatever it took. Nothing and no one was ever going to say again that *I* was holding me back.

Private transportation was arranged for our trip from Manhattan to the Bronx. The Balfours lived in the Moore Housing Project on 149th Street in the South Bronx. Going from the Jenkins's upscale apartment, to the Roberts's beautiful townhouse, to the projects in the South Bronx was unreal. I tried not to walk into the apartment building with a bad attitude. I was grateful to have a place to stay; I had just been kicked out of somebody's house with my little brother—but was this really where we were going to be living?

The building didn't look so bad from the outside, and I pretended, for the sake of Mr. Pointer, as if I didn't smell the weed when we walked into the lobby. But as soon as we got into the elevator, the stench of urine was so strong that I had to catch my breath. Thank God, our new foster care mother lived on the fourth floor so the elevator ride didn't last long. As I got on the elevator, I was wondering what Mr. Pointer must be thinking. Would he live here? Whatever his thoughts were, he kept them to himself.

A tall woman wearing a twisted wig and crooked glasses answered his knock. I stood there in disbelief. *This can't be happening*, I thought.

"Come on in," she said.

Oh, no. I was hoping she would say something more along the lines of "I'm sorry, but you obviously have the wrong apartment."

No such luck. I considered my options as she and my social worker chattered away. *Just tell me I get to register my own self for school. That is all I want to hear. I promise I'll get the best grades, if you promise never to show up at my school,* I thought.

The apartment was dreary and had the distinction of being the first roach-infested place in which I had ever lived. I wanted to run back to the Jenkins's house, but I couldn't. This was going to be my home now, and there was nothing I could do about it. There weren't a whole lot of options for two kids our ages. The Balfours were natives of the Virgin Islands. They had two grown children living elsewhere, and they were considered "professional" foster parents. Countless foster children had come in and out of their door, including one they had adopted permanently—Anthony, who was a kid about my age.

Our status was clear from the outset. Mr. and Mrs. Balfour were not going to treat Keith and me as well as they treated their adopted son. I guess the underlying message was "Don't get too comfortable, you won't be here that long." Anthony went to Catholic school. Keith and I were enrolled in a nearby public school. Anthony had his own room. Keith and I shared one. All of the candy, cookies, and other goodies were locked up in the hallway closet. Anthony had the key. We didn't. It was, without question, his home and not ours.

We moved in with the Balfours during the holiday season. I was really looking forward to a Christmas like the ones we had had with the Jenkinses, with a tree and a living room filled with neatly wrapped presents. However, Keith and I awoke on Christmas morning to find not one thing under the tree for us. Mrs. Balfour said that we had come a little too late for her to get us anything.

"I do my Christmas shopping during the summer, when prices are low," she said.

At first, I thought she was joking, but she was dead serious. My brother and I just stared at each other. What had we done to deserve this? Wasn't it bad enough that my birthday, which had just past on November 21, had been ruined?

I saw my therapist, Dr. Lewis, a lot more frequently during my stay with the Balfours. During one visit in March, I had an experience that would change my life. The receptionist at the Catholic Home Bureau noticed that my last name was the same as that of a woman sitting in the reception area. Out of curiosity, she asked the woman if she knew a Shane and Keith Salter. Well, not only did she know us, but she said that we were her grandchildren.

When I arrived for my appointment a few minutes later, the receptionist grabbed me as soon as I got off the elevator.

"Shane, Shane, your grandmother is here!"

"What?" I asked, completely puzzled.

I didn't know what to think, because I had never met my grandmother. No one had ever talked to me about her, and she wasn't a part of any of my childhood memories.

I was confused and nervous as the receptionist led me to a short, plump woman who stood up and said, "Shane, I'm your grandmother.

And this is your sister," she said, pointing to the toddler standing beside her.

Shocked and elated, I hugged my grandmother, sinking happily into her soft bosom. It was the most comforting and sincere hug I had ever experienced. It seemed so real, so natural, and so right. Memories of my early childhood came flooding back, and so did the unanswered questions about all those years.

"Do I have a brother named Peter?" I asked.

"No, but you have an uncle who is only six years older than you named Pierre," she said.

"I remember him, Grandma, I remember him. All these years, I thought he was my brother. We must have spent a lot of time together."

"You sure did, Shane," she said.

I had once thought that my grandmother was a dark, thin, silver-haired woman with a Caribbean accent who used to feed me a lot of red rice, and I asked Grandma who that woman had been.

"Oh, that's Ms. Turner. She was a sweet lady who lived in our building. She used to babysit you."

I was so excited that I was practically babbling.

"I remember the building I lived in. It had yellow brick and a fire escape outside the window."

She seemed genuinely impressed and shocked by how much I remembered.

Meanwhile, Mr. Pointer called the receptionist to ask if I had arrived for my appointment. That's when the receptionist casually mentioned that I was sitting in the lobby talking with my grandmother and sister. Well, I guess that meeting was not supposed to happen, because the next thing I knew, social workers were swooping in from every direction. They hustled me into one room and took my grandmother to another. Obviously, someone had made a big mistake, because my grandmother and I were not supposed to be at the agency at the same time.

They rushed me into a special session with Dr. Lewis to help me "process" the experience.

She asked if I wanted to get to know my grandmother and sister.

"Of course," I said.

"Okay, we'll see if we can arrange that," Dr. Lewis said.

Understandably, I had a million questions—one of which would define the rest of my life.

"Where is my mother?"

I had not forgotten her. I remembered her smell. I remembered her complexion. I remembered her songbird voice and how she had sung to me. After all those years, I was still clinging to hope that someday Mom and I would be reunited.

I actually thought that my mom was crazy and locked up in an institution somewhere. I reasoned that, because I was seeing a shrink, I must be crazy and that I had probably inherited my craziness from her. But she hadn't been institutionalized. Dr. Lewis told me that my mother was dead.

Neither one of us made a sound. We both just sat there and looked at each other. Dr. Lewis knew what to expect. I didn't. My heart sank, and a tear fell. I turned my head away and looked at the wall, staring at the play I'd written in elementary school and given to Dr. Lewis as a gift. She'd framed it and proudly displayed it all that time. *The Adopted Child* had been written when I had still had hope of being with my mother again, and now that hope was gone. I would never be able to let her know that I was doing okay and that I would grow up strong and would look after her just as I'd been looking after Keith. I would never be able to ask her why she had never come back.

The only question I could ask Dr. Lewis was "When is the funeral?" At least then, I could say my last good-bye.

At that point, Dr. Lewis reached around her desk and took my hand.

"Shane, your mother died three months ago on December 16. We didn't tell you, because it was less than a month after your adoption by the Robertses fell through. We just didn't think you could handle the news at that time. You were going through so much."

"And I'm not now?" I jabbed sarcastically. I was so hurt and angry. "How could you let them keep that from me? Why didn't somebody tell me that my mother died? I should have been allowed to go to the funeral. No one had the right to withhold that kind of information. I only had one mother, and I should have been able to say good-bye."

They'd stolen that moment, and I could never get it back.

I went back to the Balfours that afternoon, sobbing bitterly, and told my foster mother of three months all of the news that I had received that day. I was sad, confused, and angry. I desperately needed her to comfort me, hold me, and help me make sense of all that had happened that day. In a single afternoon, I had met my grandmother, discovered I had a sister, and learned that my mother was dead.

Apparently, Mrs. Balfour decided that a scathing critique of my mother would help me more than the sympathy of a caring parent would.

"You have no reason to cry about your mother's death, because she never did anything for you anyway," she snapped. "If you all were my children, we would have survived off of bread and water and stayed together as a family."

I could not believe my ears. Her words crushed me and left me not knowing what to feel. All I wanted was to be hugged and made to feel—if only for that moment—that I was not just a foster child. I needed love, compassion, and comforting. Because no one but my own mother had ever held me—not even Mrs. Jenkins, I didn't know why I had decided to confide in Mrs. Balfour. *Why did I set myself up like that?* I asked myself. *Never again*, I decided. *Shouldn't I be used to comforting myself by now?*

A few days after meeting my grandmother for the first time, I learned that she had acquired the means to take care of Keith and me and to get us out of foster care. She had been offered a larger, subsidized apartment with room enough for her, my sister, Keith, and me.

She refused the offer.

Words cannot express the horrible pain and disappointment I felt. I was told that she felt it was just too much, and I was left to wonder why. *What was wrong with me? Maybe if I were just a little better behaved, just a little cuter, just a little smarter, maybe then she would want me. Maybe somebody would want me to be his or her kid.*

It became painfully clear that during all the time that I had been separated from them, my family could have found me. They just hadn't wanted to. Even with the offer of additional housing and resources, my grandma did not want me. She sent us back, just like everyone else had. She could have at least tried it out for a while.

♦ ♦ ♦

One day about a year or so later, Grandma introduced me to a soft-spoken man with bright eyes. He was her dad. *Wow,* I thought, *this is my great-grandfather.* I couldn't believe I had a great-grandfather. All of my foster parents had been in their forties or older. I didn't know that great-grandfathers really existed.

What was most special about meeting him was something he said to me. He didn't just give me the standard "I'm so happy to see you. I remember when you were in diapers" line. I'd heard that enough times from the family members and friends that Grandma had introduced me to, and I had quickly learned that it had little meaning. They remembered me when I was in diapers, because that's all they could remember.

However, Great-Granddad said, "Shane, I always thought about you. I hoped I'd live to see this day. Here." And he pulled out a white, wrinkled, little baby shoe with my name and birthday written in faded blue ink on the side.

He said, "I made your mother give me one of your first baby shoes, because I knew there was something special about you. See, you were born the night before President Kennedy was killed. The only baby born at that time at your hospital up there in the Bronx."

"Wow, you remember that, Great-Granddad?" I said excitedly.

"It was late at night, and your mother almost died giving birth to you. In fact, she received her last rites. She was only fifteen years old. They said she wasn't going to make it, but she did. She made it, and you made it, but we lost a president the next afternoon.

"Don't you ever forget, now, that she also went to the Quonset Hut with your grandmother to have an abortion when they first found out she was pregnant with you. I'm not trying to start nothing, but your grandmother wanted her to finish her schooling. But somebody bigger than you and I had another plan. While lying on the table as they were getting ready to start the procedure, she jumped up suddenly and flew out of there."

He put his hand on my shoulder, looked me in the eye, and said, "I didn't know then—and I don't know now—what you're destined to be, but I do know this, son. Your life is destined for greatness.

"I have been saving this shoe for you all these years. Your mother would want you to have it now that you and I have been reunited. Because all your baby pictures got lost in that awful fire several years ago, hold on to this shoe. It will keep you close to your mother and will remind you where you came from and how great the struggle was to get you here."

"Thanks, Great-Granddad. I will hold on to this forever," I said.

I'd given up on believing that a family member could ever give me what I desperately needed, but he did that then. A humble man who had little material wealth, he gave me what I had been missing in my foster care relationships—a belief in my potential. He let me know that I was valued, that I mattered.

Later in our relationship, Great-Granddad told me that I shouldn't try to solve all my relatives' problems; I should get on with my own life. I couldn't hear what he was trying to say then, but I hear it now. Great-Granddad thought there was a reason that I had been removed from the family. He thought that, if I had stayed, I would never have learned the skills I needed to be the man I was supposed to be and that my life, just as I had lived it, was the perfect way to fulfill my destiny. When Great-Granddad used the word greatness, he didn't mean that everything would be easy for me or that I would be a star from the day I was born but that a transformation and redemption would emerge from the circumstances of my life. To Great-Granddad, greatness was what you did with what God gave you, trusting that God gave it to you for his glory.

Great-Granddad's appreciation for me didn't appear to be shared by my grandmother. She agreed to let Keith and me come for occasional visits, but they never lasted long.

On one of my visits, my uncle's ring came up missing. Grandma was told that I had a history of stealing, and she immediately accused me of taking it. I couldn't believe it. I would never have ruined my chance to have a relationship with my family by stealing from one of them. No matter how vehemently I insisted that I had not stolen the ring, Grandma wasn't hearing it, and she forbade Keith and me to come back to her house after that. A year later, she informed me that my uncle had misplaced the ring somewhere in the house and that it had shown up a few days after she'd thrown us out. She could have told me sooner or at least made an effort to apologize, but she didn't.

At least, my name had been cleared. That was enough for me, but it wasn't nearly enough for Keith. He was furious with Grandma for rejecting us again. My brother Keith had believed me when I told him that I hadn't stolen the ring. He always believed me. I didn't understand then how much my brother loved and looked up to me. It was hard for me to feel much of any intimate connection with anybody, even with him. I just understood the task before me; I was to make sure he was always safe. But he idolized me like no one else in my life ever could. The power I had over him as a result was incredible. I couldn't quite feel what he felt in the same way. Yet, he was everything to me. How could that be?

As we continued to grow up, it seemed he wanted from me what I was unable to give him—an emotional connection. There was just too much pain in me and too much pain between us. While he was the only one who really knew me and understood me and I was the only one who understood him, my pain was my prison, and the gap between us was beginning to get wider. He seemed to struggle with the question of why I couldn't be there for him and only him. In the midst of it all, I didn't even understand. I just knew that I had to survive for the both of us, and there was no room for feelings. But Keith didn't understand that. He expected things that I could not give, but what I gave I felt was most important. I never expected him to understand, and he never really has.

But regardless of the strain between us, he always defended me, always believed me, and always believed in me. He could not bring himself to tolerate a grandmother who would turn her back on her grandchildren. I tried to convince him to let it go, but he refused. Motivated by the desire to have a relationship with my sister, I was willing to put up with whatever I had to and to forgive whomever I needed to. I told myself that I didn't care how she felt right then. I wanted to tell her that, like the line in the Jennifer Holiday tune "I'm Not Going," sooner or later, *"you're gonna love me."* I might not have gotten the type of love I needed when I needed it, but I was determined to show all of them—through the strength of my character—that I was not only worthy of their love but that I was capable of giving love in return. I have kept working at and chasing this love for most of my life.

Learning of my mother's death and being rejected by my grandmother made me lonely, angry, and sad. I started having nightmares and became increasingly bitter toward my little brother. One night while he was asleep, I caught a roach and put it in his ear. It didn't go inside; it just crawled around the outer part of his ear, but boy, I thought it was funny watching him jump out of bed screaming. When adults weren't looking, I would slap or pinch him for no reason. I started resenting him and feeling that he was extra baggage. I was tired of looking after him. Looking after me was enough. I guess shit rolls downhill, and he was the only one I could take it out on. That is an unfair price to pay for being a little brother, and I am sorry now for my behavior toward him.

My life was spinning out of control, and I was very unhappy. I started having bouts of wrenching, burning stomach pain from all the stress. Sometimes I'd be in such agony that I would lie in bed and bite my pillow hard enough to tear the pillowcase. I told my foster mom (that twisted wig woman with the crooked glasses), but she didn't believe me. My brother would watch my suffering, and he would cry. As mean as I was to him at times, he still cared about me.

One night he just couldn't stand it anymore, and he bolted out of the bedroom and went to Mrs. Balfour to tell her how much pain I was in. She simply dismissed him.

"There's nothing wrong with Shane. Go back to your room," she said. Once again, I got no sympathy from Mrs. Balfour.

On several occasions I told my social worker, Mr. Pointer, about my stomach pains. He finally insisted that Mrs. Balfour have me evaluated by a doctor, and the doctor discovered that I was developing an ulcer. I was placed on the antacid Mylanta. I took great pleasure in saying, "I told you so," to my foster mother, but she still refused to show any sympathy for me. Instead, she was just downright mean.

"Boy, go to your room. We all have pain. My knees have been hurting me forever, and I've learned to live with it."

I hated her, and I hated living in that house. Not only did I not receive sympathy, love, or proper medical care from her, I also never had enough to eat, because Mrs. Balfour rationed our food. Fortunately, we were allowed to eat as much bread as we wanted, so I made toast all the time. When I put the bread in, the heat would make the roaches scatter from inside the toaster. It seems disgusting to me now, but I used to get such a kick out of watching the roaches scurry away. I ate so much toast in that house that now—as anyone who knows me will tell you—I do not eat bread unless I am absolutely starving and there is nothing else within driving or walking distance.

At the time, I grew sadder with each passing day. I stopped smiling altogether, because I simply had nothing to smile about, and I became increasingly evil and rebellious. I couldn't wait to find some kind of way to get out of that house. I did everything in my power to spend as little time there as possible, and I continually came in after curfew just to keep from being at home. On several occasions, I slept on the subway, riding from one end of the line to the other well into the night. Returning one night from an all-day subway ride, I knocked on the door, and Mrs. Balfour let me in. I could tell that she had something hidden behind her, but I didn't know what. The next thing I knew, she hit me over the head with a big, metal stirring spoon.

"What did you do that for?" I yelled, but she didn't answer. I was confused, in pain, and angry.

As bad as it was inside Mrs. Balfour's house, I didn't find much solace outside of it, either. While playing outside one day, I was accosted by a neighborhood gang and forced to smoke my first cigarette. They told me that if I didn't try it, they were going to rub my face in the cement. On another day, I found Keith downstairs in front of our apartment building surrounded by a crowd of Latino boys who were about to jump him. I took on three or four of those boys at one time and won. After that, I was in constant danger of being jumped in retaliation, so I had to find a place to lie low for a while.

Eventually, I found sanctuary in a dollar movie theater that was down the street that showed Bruce Lee flicks and other old movies. It was not unusual to see strange men in the theater's bathroom, masturbating at the urinals. While I was using the bathroom one day, a man standing next to me offered me money if I would leave with him. Oblivious to the danger, I followed him to his car. He unzipped my pants, fondled me, and masturbated. When he was done, he gave me a lot of money and drove me back to the theater.

I walked to my foster home, feeling horribly confused. I didn't understand why I had let that happen. I needed someone to help me make sense of it, but I certainly wasn't going to talk to Mrs. Balfour about it.

I felt so disconnected from my foster family and everyone around me that the man had been able to make me think, *Wow, here's somebody who's paying attention to me. Here's an adult who's being nice and taking an interest in me.* I felt completely dismissed at home, because Ms. Balfour's adopted son received all the love and attention that I wanted.

She didn't care where I went or what I did, so I'd had to start fending for myself in the real world, not just within the foster care system. I beat myself up over and over again, because I should not have put myself in such a situation where that man could have taken advantage of me.

But I didn't know where I belonged anymore, and I felt lost, unwanted, and vulnerable. When someone had reached out to me, tried to connect with me, I had jumped at the opportunity. It was scary how willing I was to go with anyone who, as it seemed to me, wanted to help, provide an escape, offer any kind of alternative. I had had no idea what that man had really wanted from me, what he would do to me.

I was completely confused. I'd had two sexual experiences with women, and I had been abused by my first foster sister, so I understood sexual activity, but this was different. Before, when a man had chased me in the basement and tried to abuse me, I had instinctively flown out of there. This time, I knew I'd done something terribly wrong, and it was all my fault.

This reinforced the image I had of myself as troubled and worthless. I didn't know who to talk to about the experience. There was no one, until I remembered Dr. Lewis. Thank goodness I at least had Dr. Lewis. Embarrassed and full of shame, I went to see her and told her that I was afraid that the experience meant that I was gay. She told me that I had nothing to worry about, that she worked with homosexual people in her private practice, and that what had happened to me was not a homosexual experience; it was abuse.

Fortunately, Dr. Lewis understood the underlying issue—that I was still a kid and dangerously disconnected from caring adults. At that defining moment of my life, she didn't patronize me or dismiss me, she understood that, despite the trouble I seemed to always find myself in, I was strong and intelligent, so Dr. Lewis engaged me on that level. Others seemed to ignore the reality that my childhood had been snatched from me, almost at birth. I had been forced to be the adult in my own life. I had learned how to play right along with adults, but they had mistakenly engaged me intellectually as an adult does a child.

Dr. Lewis was the only one who met me where I really was. She told me that, despite my loneliness and my isolation, I had stuff she hadn't seen in other kids. I had power to make my own choices and to chart my own destiny. She wasn't my parent; she hadn't known me on a day-to-day basis, but she had gotten to know me, and she affirmed for me that I had reason to hope. It seemed that she was the only continuity in my life, and I'm so thankful for her gift, for the hope she did give me, even during that traumatic time.

I eventually started making friends in the Balfour building, which helped me handle living in the house a little better. Two of my best friends were Robert and his sister Daphine. They were foster kids like me. Their apartment had carpet and furniture with plastic slipcovers, just like the Jenkinses had had, and their foster mother, Mrs. Barksdale, was the sweetest woman in the world. I was jealous: *Man, why didn't I get a foster home like this one?* Every time I went upstairs to their apartment, I asked Mrs. Barksdale if there was any way Keith and I could live with them. Besides having a much nicer home and decent parents, I liked the idea of living under the same roof with Daphine. I was very attracted to her, and before long, she was my girlfriend. Daphine, Robert, and I played upstairs in their room as often as we could. For me, the Barksdale house was a safe refuge, a home away from misery. But Mrs. Barksdale already had her hands full, and she knew I wasn't an easy kid, so she never agreed to let me and Keith move in.

Robert and Daphine's foster parents had a cousin named Joseph. He was in his early twenties, recently discharged from the marines, and on a fast track to become an executive at the telephone company. Joe often came by the house to see Daphine and Robert's older foster brother and sister, the Barksdales's birth children. The Barksdales told Joe about how badly the Balfours were treating me and how unhappy I was. He took an interest in me and took it upon himself to be a big brother to me.

Joe drove a sharp, late-model, navy blue Chrysler. He had a nice apartment and many well-established friends. Hanging around him exposed me to successful people and a standard of living I had not seen before. His friends became my role models. I wanted to be just like them. I got along much better with them than I did with people my age. Joe was also a great father to his little girl, and I really admired that.

Joe spent a lot of time coaching me through my problems and encouraging me to be strong. Sometimes that "be strong" stuff made me mad. *How I can be strong?* I would think to myself. *I have no one.* But Joe helped me realize that there were no other options and that I had no other choice. He had no tolerance for whining. He reminded me frequently that I was smart and that my only chance to change the direction of my life was through education.

"You have to finish school," Joe always said. "That's what matters most."

I knew that what Joe was saying was true, but it wasn't that simple. I had so much on my mind all the time. It was just too hard to concentrate in school.

How was I supposed to concentrate on schoolwork when I was hopeless, hungry, and homeless? For me, school was just another place where I didn't fit in and where no one seemed to understand me. Most of the time, I fantasized during classes about a life that was much better than the one I was living, a life in which I was actually loved and encouraged to be myself. I was getting so tired of putting on an act in order to fit in. But strangely enough, I was getting good at it.

Eventually, the things Joe said started sinking in. I started thinking, if I want nice things like he has, if I want a life like his, maybe I should take his advice.

My "big brother" Joe made me feel as if I mattered. He always kept his word and showed up when he promised. I looked up to him. At a time when my life could have gone in any direction, his interest in me was like a bridge over troubled water.

More importantly, he taught me that the best way to cross over troubled water is to count on no one other than yourself and to develop the tools necessary to build your own bridges. He kept drilling into my head that I would always be at the mercy of others if I did not have my own tools. By "tools," he meant education, communication skills, and experience. What he said was true, but I later learned that you do need to know how to depend on people every now and then during times of trouble.

♦ ♦ ♦

It was a cold, sad day when I learned that Mrs. Barksdale had had a sudden heart attack and died. Stunned, I ran upstairs to find Daphine and Robert.

As we hugged each other, Robert said, "I don't know what's going to happen to us now."

I started to cry, and all I could say was, "It'll be all right."

The morning of the funeral seemed like a bad dream. The limousine

41

and hearse were parked outside the building. Joe and the funeral directors led us downstairs for the procession to the church.

I remember Joe whispering to me, "Keep it together. Don't go making any performance."

What did he mean by that? I remember thinking. *Was I not supposed to cry? Why was I always being told to mask my emotions?*

A few days later, Daphine and Robert were moved to another foster home, and I never saw them again.

It wasn't too long afterward that, during a routine visit, Mr. Pointer asked Keith and me if we were ready to move out of Mrs. Balfour's house.

In unison and without a moment of hesitation, we both said, "Yes."

"How does living in a group home sound?" he asked.

Everything I knew about life in a group home I had learned from watching *Fish*, a popular television sitcom at the time. The kids on the show seemed to have a lot of fun, so we agreed.

There was, however, one condition: Keith and I would be separated. They couldn't send siblings to the same group home. Surprisingly, the thought of being separated was not a big deal to either of us. We were getting tired of each other anyway, or so we thought. With all the years of brotherly fights and sharing rooms, we thought it would be good to not be around each other for a while.

I knew I was tired of having him around. Carrying him was a heavy burden. I needed to be free for a while from the responsibility of looking after the two of us. I needed time to look out for myself and be on my own.

Chapter 4
LET IT BE

When I find myself in times of trouble, Mother Mary comes to me,
Speaking words of wisdom, "Let it be."
—John Lennon and Paul McCartney

My little brother Keith and I moved into separate group homes. I moved into a large group home on Lacombe Avenue in the Soundview section of the Bronx. Mr. and Mrs. Hopkins, the house parents, lived in an apartment upstairs during the week and drove to their house in Connecticut on weekends. The kitchen refrigerators had steel doors that were locked unless meals were being prepared. The home had a diverse mix of children, including some in wheelchairs, which was hard to get used to at first. However, I quickly realized that we all had a lot in common. The others had the same hopes and fears that I did. They wanted to be happy, just as I did. They were misunderstood, just as I had been. And, just like me, someone had rejected them.

I'll always remember Eric. He was born with no arms or legs. I made the mistake once of mouthing off to him, figuring that, if I could get away with being smart to anyone, it would be the kid with no arms and legs. Eric taught me a lesson or two. That dude hopped out of his wheelchair onto the floor so quickly. He picked me up with one of his upper stubs, threw me to the floor, and whipped my butt with the other stub. He quickly earned my respect. I had to learn what everyone in the house already knew: *Don't mess with Eric.* There was more strength in those short stubs than most of us had in our arms.

Another person who taught me something was Eugene. He was also in a wheelchair, because he had cerebral palsy. He was one of the smartest and most compassionate people I had ever met, and we became very close friends. He was like a brother to me.

In fact, there was a bond that transcended ethnicity or disability among all the kids in the house. That home was different from any I had ever lived in.

There was one thing, unfortunately, that being in a new home did not change; I still found a way to get into a tremendous amount of trouble. Some of the guys and I would take Eric on the train in his wheelchair. Grasping a can between his stubs, he would beg passengers for money. At the end of the day, we would equally split everything we had collected—and, boy, would we clean up!

It was also the time in my life when I started experimenting with weed, beer, and cigarettes. Hanging out with the boys one night, I put down a quart of Olde English, smoked a joint, and had my first Salem cigarette. My head was spinning so badly and my stomach was so upset that I thought I was going to die. When I got back to the group home, I tried to lie down, but the room kept spinning. I promised myself that, if I lived through the night, I would never do that again. When I woke up the next morning, I found myself on restriction—a group home term for punishment—for two weeks. I regret that it did not deter me. My desire to fit in with the boys was much greater than my fear of being punished. I just figured I would smoke and drink a little less the next time around.

During my stay at the Soundview Group Home, I developed grand mal epileptic seizures. I was stunned. I'd already been through hell in my short, fourteen-year life. Then my body was under attack by seizures that seemed to come upon me without warning and for no apparent reason. They started happening so frequently that doctors said my life was threatened. My neurological system couldn't handle so many grand mal seizures, one after the other. Anytime I had a seizure, it was just exhausting, and I'd have to spend the next day or two sleeping. The doctors put me on Dilantin, phenobarbital, and Tegretol—three very serious medications. Most epileptics only took one of those medications. The drugs weren't able to eliminate the seizures, so they continued.

One time, I had a seizure on the subway platform. None of the passengers knew what to do. One lady thought she needed to put something in my mouth, so she used her makeup mirror, which was disastrous. It cut up my mouth, and all the blood only made matters worse.

After being diagnosed with epilepsy, I was even more angry and depressed than I had been at other points in my life. The last thing I had wanted was another challenge, and then I had been diagnosed with epilepsy—something else to make me feel like a freak. It increased my feelings of insecurity and isolation and of being in danger. The seizures were also embarrassing; they exacerbated my sense that I was different.

Strangely, the seizures intensified right after I left Keith in Rochester. I'm sure it had something to do with the fact that I was not allowed to speak to him or see him. After his new foster family moved, there was no way for me to contact him, no way for me to know if he was okay, now way to tell him I was okay. I think my epilepsy was partially my body's reaction to the separation and endless worrying if leaving him behind had been the right decision. Did he need a home more than we needed each other? The consequences of my decision tore me up inside.

Then several years later, just as abruptly as they had started, my seizures went away. Before I went away to college I had an EEG, and mysteriously it came back normal, showing no brain abnormalities. Thank God, I haven't had a seizure since.

It was at Soundview that I met one of my best female friends ever. Vanessa was kind and loving, but she was also no-nonsense. She was just as tough as she was generous and would kick your butt in a minute. We never dated, but Vanessa and I developed an extremely close friendship. Vanessa introduced me to her parents, Mr. and Mrs. Moragne. I grew to like them so much—and Vanessa and I were so close—that I asked Vanessa if I could live with her family. I was so disappointed when they said I couldn't, but we all remained very close, and Vanessa and I started referring to each other as brother and sister.

I had been attending the New York High School of Printing for about a year when I auditioned for the theater program at Julia Richman High School for the Performing Arts. I was determined to fulfill my dream of becoming an actor, so I could show all those people who did not want me that I was special. I knew I had a gift for acting, and I thought it might just be a way out of my loneliness and rejection.

I jumped, screamed, and ran up and down the stairs the day I got my acceptance letter to Julia Richman. There was no doubt in my mind that I was destined to be a great movie star. Becoming a student at that highly regarded school was the first step toward fulfilling that dream.

Every day was a great day at Julia Richman. I worked hard in my acting classes, determined to perfect my craft. One of the most exciting moments from that period of my life was when MGM Studios held auditions at our school for the movie *Fame*. I auditioned for the part of Leroy, and I must have really impressed MGM, because I got a callback. However, I guess it was just not my time, because the part of Leroy went to one of my school rivals, Gene Anthony Ray. Gene was an awesome dancer with a nasty attitude; in my opinion, he could not act. Because of that view, I thought for sure that I was going to get the part, but I guess they wanted a dancer—not an actor.

At the movie's premier, I was sick with envy. I could not help but wonder what my life would be like if I were up on that movie screen playing Leroy instead of Gene. *Fame* had taken Gene out of the hood to the kind of life I wanted so badly. For me, it was back to the hood and to living in the group home.

It was not very long after that, though, that I got a different kind of ticket out of the hood. The social workers had identified another adoptive family for me. It would be in Rochester, New York, with an unmarried, Baptist minister.

Reverend Cameron had already successfully adopted a six-year-old boy. That record of accomplishment gave me hope that, perhaps this time, an adoption would finally work for Keith and me. However, Keith wanted no part of family living again. The thought of being with a family again and then of being rejected was just too painful. The Jenkinses had let him down and the Robertses had tossed us aside after two months. He decided that group-home living, without any emotional attachments, was safer. But I saw it as a chance for us to be reunited and a chance for me to take care of him the way I had before. I knew he needed me.

While we had been separated, Keith's behavior had been getting bad. He had started stealing bicycles and getting into all kinds of trouble. No one could get through to him. The social workers kept asking me to talk to Keith about his behavior, because I was the only one he would listen to. That's why I didn't want to pass up the chance for the adoption. I didn't even care that Rochester was so far away from New York City and thought maybe that was a good thing. It seemed that I had experienced nothing but pain in the Big Apple anyway, so I took charge of the situation and told Keith that we were going to do it—whether he wanted to or not. It was a chance for us to be loved, happy, and secure. Besides, we had started to miss living with each other, and I knew that deep down he wanted to be with his big brother.

In my mind, being adopted and having a family was the absolute answer to all of my troubles. I dreamed constantly of living in a big house, having a nice car, and wearing nice clothes, and I thought that having a family was a step toward getting those things. It hurt so much whenever I heard other children talk about their parents. It didn't matter whether what they said about their parents was good or bad—at least they had parents. I wanted my own mom and dad. A family would also help me do my job of protecting Keith. A family meant security, and if anything ever happened to me, he would be safe.

I realized that the clock was running out for us, because we were no longer two cuddly little boys in need of a home. We were teenagers by then, and people were not knocking down doors to take in kids like us.

On the day we met with Reverend Cameron for the first time, I whispered to Keith, "Look, man, don't blow it. Smile a lot. We have to be on our best behavior."

It worked! After a few visits, we were leaving the past behind and moving out of New York City to Rochester. I had another chance at my lifelong dream of having a family we could call our own.

Once again, we were starting fresh with a new home and a new dad. I decided that I wanted to mark the new beginning by changing my name. Somehow, I reasoned that the name Shane had brought me and everyone else around me only heartache. My new dad's only stipulation was that I had to research the meaning of my new name and write a full page to explain why I chose it. I picked the name Karim, which means "generous." My full name became Karim Abdu Jamar Cameron. Keith decided to just change his middle name from Earl to Elliott.

At our new home, I was excited to have a new little brother who had also been adopted. His name was Marcus, and we hit it off immediately. I think Keith was a little jealous of him. At the same time, Keith seemed happy to finally be a big brother and glad that he would attend the same school as Marcus: St. Louis Catholic School in Pittsford, New York.

My new dad took me on visits to choose a school. We visited two public high schools, one all-boys Catholic school, and one coed Catholic school. After touring and meeting with the principals of all four schools, he asked me to rate them in my order of preference. I thought it was so cool that he was going to let me choose. Eager to exercise the wonderful, new freedom, I quickly rated the two public high schools one and two, the Catholic coed school number three, and the all-boys Catholic school last. I turned my preferences over to Dad, who looked at them and said, "You will be attending St. Thomas Aquinas."

That was the most academically rigorous of the four—and the one with no girls. I wanted to know why he had bothered to ask my opinion, only to select the one I had chosen as my last preference. He said that St. Thomas Aquinas would be the most challenging and that he thought that black boys needed academic challenges to prepare them for manhood. Then my dad hit me with the biggie. He told me that I would start the new school in the ninth grade, although New York City Public Schools (NYCPS) had duly promoted me to the tenth grade. He said he had no confidence in the NYCPS curriculum, because the standards were inferior. Okay, I admit that my grades sucked, but I *was* passing, even though it was with Cs and Ds.

My attitude toward Reverend Cameron changed. Why did this big, fat, Afro-wearing dude think he could come into my life and tell my school to make me repeat a grade? As if that was not bad enough, I had to cut off my long-awaited mustache, because the school did not allow boys to have facial hair. From that moment on, I was convinced that he was crazy; group home living looked like paradise. At least there I had been able to make my own decisions.

There was no changing my dad's mind about how things were going to be. I was enrolled at the predominantly white St. Thomas Aquinas. I made friends quickly, especially with the few black kids who were there. All of them had come from very good homes with strong values. They followed the rules, did their homework on time, and stayed out of trouble.

One kid stood out from the others. He appeared unhappy and angry and acted as if he did not want to be there. He was the school's notorious "bad boy," so naturally, I wanted to be friends with him. I was actually afraid of him until we discovered that we had a lot in common. Neither of us was living with our parents, and Kevin's parents were struggling with substance abuse the way my mother had. Kevin and I were drawn to each other and hit it off right from the start. Meeting him was like a ray of sunshine coming through prison bars. I kept my other friends, but I wasn't as close to them as I was to Kevin. While we were cool at school and would hang out at dances, I never went over to anyone else's house but Kevin's to hang out. Kevin and I understood hard times.

My new dad felt like a jail guard. He screened my letters from my grandmother, my friend Vanessa, her parents, and other folks from New York City. He forbade me to remain in contact with my family and New York friends, saying it was out of concern for the kind of influence they might have over me while I was adjusting to my new home. I didn't understand his rationale. I was mad and felt cut off from the world I'd known all of my life. The more he tried to make me forget my past, the more I longed to hold on to it.

Though, there was one positive: with Dad's permission, I decided to join the school band.

"What instrument do you want to play?" Dad asked.

"The teacher said he has space only in the percussion section, so I can play either the drums or the xylophone."

"I didn't ask you what the band instructor said. I asked *you* what instrument *you* want to play."

"I've always wanted to play the trombone."

"Then that's what you'll play," he declared.

As he drove me to the music shop that night, I wondered how I was going to just show up at school with a trombone when the teacher had said that there was only room in the percussion section.

The next day, Dad went to school with me and spoke privately with the band teacher. I don't know what he said, but I played the trombone in the band that year. Now that was cool. I had never had anyone go to bat for me like that before. *Is this what it means to be somebody's kid?* I wondered. *Is this what real parents do for their children?* All I knew for sure was that, at that moment, I felt special. It almost made up for all the ways he was so strict with me.

On another occasion, the school sent a note home that said that

I had to shave off my little peach fuzz of a mustache. Once again, my dad stood up for me, and I became one of the only kids in school who didn't have to shave. By then, in my eyes, Dad had more than redeemed himself. I was once again beginning to dig this family thing.

Meanwhile, Keith and I worked at living with each other once more, though we weren't doing a great job at it. We started having fights over the pettiest things. One Sunday after church, I flew into a rage over socks—I noticed that my white tube socks were damaged beyond repair.

No matter how many times I tell Keith not to wear my clothes, he never listens, I fumed. *Dad doesn't do anything to Keith when he does something wrong, so Keith just does whatever he wants.*

After a few minutes of egging myself on, I was furious, and before I knew it, I was screaming at the top of my lungs, "I'm so sick of this shit!"

I'm not sure if it was the fact that I cursed or the fact that I cursed on a Sunday, but my dad came flying into the room and slapped me upside my head.

Shocked, angry, and extremely embarrassed, I ran upstairs and locked myself in my room. I lay across the bed for what seemed like hours, growing more distraught about my life with every minute. *This adoption is going down the tubes fast,* I decided. *They always like Keith better than me.* I reached the conclusion that I couldn't do anything right.

I hated myself. That home was not the dream that I had thought it would be, and I had already failed at adoption once. All I had ever wanted was a family, and I just couldn't take any more hurt and rejection. I couldn't deal with being misunderstood and unaccepted anymore. What other choice was there for me? Life was hopeless, and I didn't see the use of going on.

I decided that the best course of action was to kill myself. I looked at my Dilantin, and without hesitation, swallowed all of the pills. As I sat on my bed, my eyes got heavy, and I became extremely groggy. Convinced that I was on my way to certain death, I reconsidered, and stumbled downstairs to tell Dad what I had done. He hustled Keith, Marcus, and me into the car and rushed to the hospital.

The emergency room physician chastised me for trying to take my life.

"Nothing could be that bad," he said.

"Oh, yes, it could," I mumbled under my breath. "Living with my dad is hell."

As they were getting the pills out of my system, I overheard Dad say to the doctors and nurses that he wanted this to be a miserable and unforgettable experience for me. Against medical advice, he signed me out of the hospital. On the way home, he stopped at a steak house and parked the car near the kitchen, where I could fully experience the nauseating aroma of food cooking.

The next morning, despite having been at the hospital extremely late, Dad woke me up bright and early for school. When we arrived at school, he walked me into the principal's office and issued clear instructions to the faculty that I was to attend all classes regardless of how I felt. Although the school usually respected his wishes, when they learned what I'd been through the night before, they let me go to the guidance counselor's office, where I slept for most of the day. I felt vindicated. Even the school felt Dad was being unreasonable. In my mind, the same father who had made me feel special by standing up for me had turned completely against me.

Okay, I get the message, I thought. *Maybe attempting to kill myself is something I'll think twice about next time, but if this mental anguish keeps up, I'll finish what I started.*

My dad had a very different way of viewing how things should be done than most other people. Everything was either black or white. As a teenager, this seemed so different from most other adults. His unconventional perspective started making me unpopular at school. After a few weeks of checking my homework, he decided that I wasn't bringing home a sufficient amount.

"Oh, this won't work," he said. "I'll have to let them know that I'm paying too much tuition for them to be sending this nonsense home and calling it homework."

And that's exactly what he did. As a result, the homework load for the entire class doubled, and somehow it got out that that was the direct result of my dad's actions. I caught much grief from the entire class, including my friend Kevin.

When Dad found out that I was friends with bad boy Kevin, he told me not to associate with him during school so I could focus fully on my academic priorities. Kevin and I started talking on the phone late into the night to compensate for the fact that we couldn't talk at school anymore. One night, we talked until two am about everything from sex to drugs, not knowing that my dad was eavesdropping.

The next morning, all hell broke loose. Dad jumped all over me and forbade me from having any contact with Kevin ever again. He even asked Kevin's grandmother to help him enforce his new rule, but fortunately, she ignored him and continued to let me hang out with Kevin at her place.

When the nearby all-girls school partnered with our all-boys school to have a dance, Dad insisted on meeting my date beforehand—before I could call someone a friend, he had to approve. The night of the dance, my date's parents dropped her off at my house where I introduced her to Dad. Well, she seemed to pass inspection, because he allowed us to leave for the dance without any objections. After I got home from a fantastic evening, Dad said that he disapproved of my date because she hadn't stood up to greet him. *How ridiculous*, I thought. Living with that man was just getting to be too much. With each day that passed, I was growing more and more resentful of Dad. If that was what having a father meant, then maybe I didn't need one.

I started complaining about him to anyone who'd listen. Even the adults I confided in agreed that he was simply too unreasonable.

Finally, I decided it was time to get away from Reverend Cameron for good. I ran away to Kevin's house with no intention of ever returning. Regrettably, that was the first place Dad looked for me, and he had me back home in a matter of a few hours. I ran away several more times after that, and each time, Dad called the same big, black police officer to fetch me home.

Determined to finally run away and not be caught, I saved enough money to get a bus ticket back to New York City. I had several hours before my bus was scheduled to leave, so I called Dad's mother, Grandma Cameron. She asked me where I was, but I wouldn't tell her, fearing she'd blab to Dad. She told me that she felt bad about how unreasonable my father was being and implied that she understood what I was going through. My defenses were lowered by her empathy, and somehow, I really did think I could trust her. I told her where I was, and she offered to take me to her place to get some sleep before I got on the bus the next morning. On the way to her house, Grandma stopped by Dad's house "just to get your pajamas," she promised.

She had me duck down in the backseat so Dad couldn't see me. She retrieved the pajamas, and we were on our way. About thirty minutes after arriving at Grandma's, the doorbell rang. To my surprise, it was Dad and the same police officer who had chased me down so many times before.

"Shane, do you think I have nothing better to do but chase you around Rochester?" the officer quipped.

"As long as you keep sending me back to his house, you are going to have to keep chasing me," I said.

I didn't know then that I would never go back there.

They took me to a place called Hillside Children's Center. It was a cold place with heavy metal doors that locked tight behind me as I entered the building. They told me that I would be staying at Hillside for two weeks and that Dad was forbidden to see me while counselors helped me work out my problems.

After I showered and was processed in, I met with some people who wanted information from me. I hesitated, because I wasn't sure why they wanted it. Who were they going to share it with? Although every time I talked to a counselor or most other adults, they promised to keep the things I shared secret, I finally figured out by the time I was fifteen that promises were things that adults just didn't keep. Somehow I still trusted my therapist Dr. Lewis, but she was in New York City, and I was behind bars in a residential treatment facility. *Maybe I am really crazy*, I thought some nights as I stared aimlessly at the wall. *I should have killed myself* was the alternating thought.

The place was at least clean, and I had a lot of quiet time to think about my life and my dreams, fears, and pain. I was sad but not angry. Sad because I didn't want to blow a good family for my brother, but I knew I couldn't give up the fight for my own life.

By the second week at Hillside and without saying a word to anyone, I figured out my problem, and I cried, and I cried. Although I wanted a family as much as I wanted life itself, I discovered that it was too late for me. It was too late, because I was convinced that no adult could do a better job of raising me than me. In that facility, without my freedom, I discovered that the very thing required to succeed in a family was the very thing I wasn't willing to do: give up control. My job was to let all of them know that I couldn't do the family thing on somebody else's terms. *When I leave the gates of Hillside, I will go back to being in control*, I concluded.

At the end of the two weeks, a Rochester social worker and my social worker from New York City, Mr. Pointer, met with my dad and me. They asked if I wanted to go back to Dad's house. I quickly responded with a firm, "No!" They said that Dad wanted me home and was willing to change some of his parenting techniques.

Yeah, he might change, but I doubt it, I thought. I didn't want to take that chance. I told them that there was no way I would ever go back. I looked up and was shocked to see a tear fall from my dad's eye. Seeing him cry for the first time made me think about staying with him, but I couldn't give in. In fact, a part of me wanted to cause him as much pain as I could.

I looked him straight in the eye and spoke words that I hoped would hurt him as all my parents before him had hurt me.

"I'm fifteen, and you're twenty-five. What makes you think you can ever be my father?"

Everyone stared at me in disbelief. I just stared right back, determined not to display any trace of sadness.

"Reverend Cameron is willing to keep your brother Keith, whether you stay or not," someone said.

"If Keith has a chance to have a family, that's great. No problem. I am not going to stand in the way," I said. Besides, Keith was not having the same problems I was. He was a good kid.

Then Dad said something that truly pierced my heart.

"If you leave, there's no coming back. And you can never see or talk to Keith again."

Swallowing an orange-size lump in my throat, I looked at him and everyone else in the room and said, "If that's what it takes, no problem."

Tears fell down my face as the magnitude of my decision sank in. I had agreed to leave my brother behind, which meant leaving my heart and a piece of my soul behind. Without Keith, what was my purpose for living? My biggest accomplishment so far was being his parent. It had been my life task. But he was safe. He had a family. I admitted to myself that, perhaps, I was a bad influence on him. Maybe Keith would be better off without me. I knew I needed to focus on getting my life straight then. At that moment, I accepted the reality that my dream of having a family would never materialize.

As awful as that realization was, I knew it was true. There would be no more trying to hit targets that kept moving, no more trying to be cute enough to win over families, no more trying to behave well enough not to be kicked out of one. I saw some dreams just could not be. From that moment on, I knew that I was all that I had, and I was determined to survive.

My eyes were red and swollen from crying by then, but Mr. Pointer knew my mind was made up.

"Well, Shane, how do you want to travel back to New York City?"

"I've never been on a plane before," I confessed, my voice quivering.

Once again, Mr. Pointer was there to help me pick up the broken pieces of my life. He was more than a social worker to me; he was like family. It was obvious from day one that he really cared about me. For some odd reason, he thought I had potential. He really believed in me and believed me. When I was sad, he would be standing to the side, fighting back tears, but he was also a tough, no-nonsense guy. I never quite figured out how to manipulate him. Mr. Pointer gave me only so much rope before yanking it back.

Doing his best to console me and lift my spirits, he said, "Then let's fly back, Shane."

And we did.

The flight from Rochester to New York City was my first airplane ride, and it was very exciting. But once we landed, reality set in—Mr. Pointer didn't have a place for me to stay when I returned to New York City. He asked me if I had any ideas.

"How about the Moragnes?" I suggested.

"Why don't you call them and see if they would be willing to be an emergency foster home for you?"

I called Vanessa, and she asked her parents, who promptly agreed to take me in for a while. They had never liked Reverend Cameron anyway.

Chapter 5
THE DREAM WITH MY NAME ON IT

"Small one," my mama said, "your life has just begun.
You see the range of stormy weather,
But there's rainbows there, and things will soon get better,
So hang on, 'cause there is a dream out there with your name on it."
— Jennifer Holliday

Back in New York City, I was determined to make the most of my life.
I had two failed adoptive placements under my belt, but I wanted to
prove something to myself and to all those who had repeatedly said I'd
never amount to anything. Fortunately, the Moragnes were willing to
give me a place to stay while Mr. Pointer and I sorted things out. The
Moragnes lived in Mitchell Houses, one of the better public housing
developments. I didn't smell urine in the elevators as much as I had in
some of the others, and it wasn't roach-infested.

My return to New York was obviously emotionally difficult. I had
been separated from my brother again and had to accept that I would
likely never see or speak to him again. My seizures started coming with
greater frequency and intensity, so that I was in and out of the hospital
all the time. At one point, the seizures were occurring so often that the
neurologist expressed serious concern about their effect on my nervous
system. It was clear what was happening—I was grieving for my brother
and the lost relationship with a father as if they had both died, and my
body was reacting to that grief.

I would not have made it through all of that without Pop Moragne.
He and I really connected, and his presence had a comforting and
calming influence on me. While the social workers were completing

the paperwork so the Moragnes could become my long-term foster parents, doctors discovered that Mom Moragne had been exposed to tuberculosis. That meant that I had to be immediately removed from their home. Thanks to a positive TB test, I was going to have to leave a place where I finally felt comfortable and had been accepted unconditionally.

"This can't be happening," I groaned. I was beginning to think I shouldn't bother to unpack. Whenever I moved to someplace new, I was never there long. I hated having to leave the Moragnes, but I had no choice.

Mr. Pointer was able to find yet another foster family for me, this time in the Bushwick section of Brooklyn. Mr. and Mrs. Edwards had a son and a daughter. They also had a teenage foster child named Fritz living with them. It was clear from the very beginning that they planned to adopt Fritz and that they had no interest in adopting me. What foster parent wouldn't have wanted to adopt Fritz? He was easygoing, didn't talk back, and helped around the house. The closest thing he had to a vice was an occasional basketball game. I, unfortunately, was nothing like Fritz.

Mr. and Mrs. Edwards were devout Roman Catholics. The house was filled with statues of Mary, Jesus, and Joseph. There was a strong Muslim community in the neighborhood as well. Although I was growing up under the supervision of a Catholic agency and I'd had strong Catholic influences from the Jenkins family, I had always been impressed and intrigued by Muslims. They were so neatly dressed and seemed so disciplined. I started thinking that maybe self-discipline was what was missing in my life. Maybe if I were more disciplined, I could focus better in school. Maybe if I focused in school, I would achieve my goals, just as my big brother Joe had always said I should. I started paying a lot more attention to the Muslims—the way the women revealed only their eyes and the way the men draped themselves in clothing from head to toe. When a man's head was exposed, he always had a very neat, close-tapered haircut. To me, they stood out and represented themselves well.

On my way home one day, I stopped into the neighborhood mosque. I talked with some of the brothers there, and as I learned more about Islam, I became excited about belonging somewhere. I decided to have my Shahada (the equivalent of Christian baptism). I selected a Muslim name: Elijah Abdullah Kareem Abdula Muhammad (or EAKAM for short). I told the brothers of the Ansar Allah Community that I was homeless. I had a place to sleep with a foster family, but it wasn't really home for me. I told them that the Catholic Home Bureau was my guardian and that none of the homes they had found for me had worked out. I asked the brothers if they would adopt me and let me grow up as a Muslim.

The brothers welcomed me. They said they were willing to adopt me and that they would be happy to have my social worker visit their community to determine if it was a suitable place for me to live. They even said they would send me to college if my grades were good enough, but they would decide my field of study based on the needs of the community. That probably meant that my career in theater was out of the question. However, for what I'd get in return—safety, security, discipline, and a permanent home—I thought it was a good tradeoff. Besides, I had felt drawn to the Muslims for quite some time. I was sure that that was the right place for me.

I returned to Mrs. Edwards that day dressed as a new Muslim, wearing all white and feeling euphoric.

When Mrs. Edwards opened the door, she looked as if she had seen a ghost. She pulled herself together long enough to ask, "Did any of the neighbors see you coming down the street?" She seemed quite frazzled. Apparently, the sight of me in Muslim clothing had sent her over the edge. "I can't take any more of this. They're going to have to do something with you. I can't have you around here dressed like that," she said.

Mrs. Edwards phoned Mr. Pointer and told him that I had to go immediately. I don't know what Mr. Pointer said, but she calmed down and handed me the phone. I told Mr. Pointer that I had asked the Muslims to adopt me and that they had said they would. He immediately set up an appointment to visit the mosque.

I don't know what happened during Mr. Pointer's visit to the Ansar Allah Community, but it definitely had an effect on him. He told me that, if I ever went back there, I would be sent straight to Juvenile Hall. I supposed he thought that would be the end of it, but I refused to accept his decision. I was furious that the agency was not willing to honor my wishes. How dare they? With all the horrible placements I'd endured throughout my life, they were denying me a welcoming new family. I knew enough to realize that I had the constitutional right to practice the religion of my choice, and I called the New York Legal Aid Society for help. I explained to the woman who answered the phone that I was a foster child under the guardianship of the Catholic Home Bureau and that I had just become a Muslim.

"Don't I have a constitutional right to freedom of religion?" I asked.

I could not have been more disappointed when she told me that as long as I was a ward of the state, the state was my guardian, and I had to do what they said. I could practice whatever religion I wanted when I turned eighteen. That's when it hit me that I was the property of New York State and that the state controlled my every move. Whether I wanted to or not, I had to accept Mr. Pointer's decision.

I never went back to the mosque again.

Thankfully, Mrs. Edwards got over being upset that I had become a Muslim and decided to allow me to remain in her home until other arrangements could be made for me. I was happy to have a place to stay, but what I really wanted was to be out of foster care, to be on my own, and to make my own decisions. The decisions other people made for me just seemed to hold me back. I was sure I could do better. For then, however, it was back to stay with the Edwards family.

The Bushwick neighborhood wasn't a very safe part of Brooklyn. In retrospect, I probably shouldn't have been riding the subway alone to school and to visits with my social worker. One day while I was returning home after seeing Mr. Pointer, excited about new eyeglasses that I had bought with money I had saved from my summer job at the social services department, a deranged man attacked me.

I'd noticed him loudly babbling to himself earlier when I had gotten on the train, but I didn't pay him much attention, because people often talk to themselves on the subway. He switched seats several times while the train emptied until there were less than a handful of people in the car. The next thing I knew, he had cornered me in my seat and was hitting me. The first punch broke my new glasses. All I could do was cover my face and curl up like a baby as the man pounded his fists into my back and head. I wondered why no one would help me. It began to feel like, at that point in my life, there wasn't anybody to help me.

A white-haired old woman attempted to intervene on my behalf. I heard a voice asking him, "Why are you doing this to a little boy? He didn't do anything to you."

For a moment I felt relieved, until he said, "Bitch, mind your own business before I kick your ass."

She retreated to the far end of the train, and he continued to hit me.

The beating went on and felt like it took forever. All I could do was close my eyes and hope he wouldn't kill me. As with everything else in my life, I eventually became numb and left my body.

As the train pulled into the next station, he suddenly stopped beating me, and I ran from the train and found the conductor. I asked him to help and told him I was an epileptic and afraid I would have a seizure.

His only response was, "If I were you, I'd go back and kick his ass." My saving grace was a police officer standing on the platform. When I explained what had happened, he followed me back onto the train, handcuffed my attacker, and led us to a back room in the subway station.

With the door shut, the police officer took out his club and beat the living daylights out of the man. After administering several hard blows, he paused and asked me if I had seen anything.

"No," I said, so he continued to pummel the guy. As my attacker screamed in pain, the officer kept calling him a punk for picking on a little kid. Although I was bruised and beaten, I was conflicted by the beating he withstood. Somehow, it just seemed wrong to me. For a moment, though, I must admit that I thought he deserved it, too.

♦ ♦ ♦

While living with the Edwards family, I decided to try to strengthen my relationship with my grandmother. She had rejected me repeatedly, but I was determined not to abandon one of the few relationships I had with blood relatives. I started visiting her more frequently, and in the process, began developing a relationship with my uncle Johnny. Everyone was afraid of Uncle Johnny, because he had served a long sentence in a facility for the criminally insane. Almost everyone in the family avoided him, except me. I liked him. He got very excited whenever I visited and would ask me to read the Bible to him. At the time, he and his sister, Cookie, were the only people in the family who made me feel wanted. I later learned from Grandma that Johnny had been my mom's favorite brother.

One day, I arrived at my grandmother's house to find a tall man visiting her. Grandma introduced him as her old boyfriend, Vernon. She introduced me as Dee Dee's son.

Dee Dee's son? Who's Dee Dee? I wondered to myself.

Seeing the puzzled look on my face, Grandma said, "Sit down, Shane."

I figured something big was about to be revealed, and I was right. Grandma told me that Vernon was my birth father's brother.

"Your dad's name is David," she continued. "Dee Dee is a nickname."

That's when Vernon spoke up: "This is Shane? Oh my God! I haven't seen you since you were in diapers!"

The news was shocking, but it felt so good to meet someone who remembered me. I was even more delighted to learn that he knew where my father was.

"Would you tell him I'd like to see him?" I asked, trying hard to contain my excitement.

"Oh, he wants to see you too," Vernon said.

I couldn't believe it. Someone knew where my father was, and my father wanted to see me! It was all I could do not to jump up and down screaming. I asked Uncle Vernon to ask my father to get in touch with me right away.

That day, I left Grandma's extremely happy. That one visit alone had given me more hope than I'd had in years that I would finally find one person in the world who really wanted me.

The next day, the phone rang before daylight, and it was my father.

"Hello. Shane?"

My heart was racing. "Yes. This is Shane."

"Oh my God!" he screamed. "It's my son!"

His excitement was exhilarating. I could feel how genuinely thrilled he was to find me.

"I have thought about you every day," he said. "I love you, son. I've always loved you," he told me. He said he had tried to find me but that everyone had lied to him about where I was. They'd even lied to him about my name.

"I thought your name was David," he said. "When can I see you?"

"How about today?"

Before I could hang up the phone, my dad was on his way. I couldn't believe it. As a little boy, I had fantasized about meeting my father. I had imagined that he was rich and that my being in foster care was just a big mistake. I couldn't wait to see what he was really like.

A few hours later, he arrived.

Right away, I realized he wasn't going to live up to my rich father fantasy. He was driving a loud, rusty, beat-up, old car. He didn't even bother to park it. He threw open the door and practically leapt out. We ran to meet one another, and he grabbed me and lifted me off the ground. He held me and kept saying over and over again, "My son, my son," and he cried.

He ain't rich, and he ain't tall, I thought. *But he is my father.* That was enough for me. I searched his face, looking for the family resemblance. We looked alike. *Finally, after all these years, I look like somebody else,* I thought. When we finally let go of each other, I noticed a very attractive woman stepping from the passenger side of the car.

"This is Joanne," he said proudly.

I was thinking that my dad had really good taste in women, when he asked me if I wanted to ride with them to his apartment. I immediately said yes.

We piled into the rickety old car and started out for Dad's place in the Fort Apache section of the Bronx. I was so thrilled that I couldn't stop talking on the drive over. I wanted to tell him everything that had ever happened to me. Who knew if we would ever have this chance again? I listened closely to his every word too, hoping to find out as much about him and my family as I could. There was no question that he wouldn't answer. We were both so excited.

His rusty, old car was extremely noisy, so we had to talk loudly. That was okay; I was with my father. I could put up with a little noise.

However, what I saw when we pulled up to his place really tested my tolerance. My father lived in a condemned building. Most of the apartments had been vacated, and wires were running from one apartment to the next to share electricity. There were plenty of rats and roaches, but there was no hot water. The ceiling was caving in, and the walls were filthy. Unbelievably though, after a while, I didn't care. He was my father, and I wanted to be wherever he was. I told him I was not going back to my foster home and that I wanted to stay with him.

"This is your home, son. You don't have to go back."

His words made me so happy that I was speechless. All I could do was hug him and cry.

I moved in with Dad right away, and we started to get better acquainted. I was quite surprised when he told me that I had sixteen brothers and sisters. The woman he had married had had three children before she had died; David Jr., Adrienne, and Debbie were being raised by their maternal grandmother. Another of my sisters lived with relatives in the Caribbean. The rest were in foster care or adopted. He said they knew about me and that he couldn't wait for me to meet them all.

I had been living with my father for just a few days when it was time for my subway assault case to be heard in court. It felt great having Dad go to court with me. He wanted to see who had attacked his son. My chest poked out so far I almost busted my buttons. *My father will kick your butt if you mess with me*, I mouthed to myself as we sat in the courtroom together. I felt protected like I never had before.

At last, I felt safe, and the outcome of the case was also good. The judge ruled that my attacker had to stay away from me for six months and had to pay victim's compensation for the glasses he had broken.

Outside the court, my father confronted the man and told him what he'd do to him if he ever saw him again. That small act made my father my hero.

However, just like almost every other good thing in my life to that point, my fantasy of what life would be like with my real family was quickly destroyed. I found out that my father made a living selling stolen toys and bootlegged VHS tapes on the street. He thought I would be a natural at selling things, so he took me with him on several occasions. I never really wanted to go. I wanted him to make an honest living. At the same time, I wanted to be with him, so I made an effort to understand his world.

As the days passed, his world kept getting scarier and scarier to me. People came knocking on the door at all hours of the night. I was never allowed to answer, and they were never invited in. Once I peeped into his bedroom and saw him scraping white powder off the folding table beside his bed. I knew enough to know it was cocaine. *Oh, my God, my father has cocaine. Is that why people are knocking at the door all night?*

As much as I didn't want it to be true, I knew then that my dad was distributing and selling drugs.

In spite of his unorthodox enterprises, my dad tried to make living with him as safe and normal as possible. He enrolled me in Alfred E. Smith High School. That meant I had to leave my friends at Julia Richman behind. It was hard to leave, because my last few months at Julia Richman had been some of my best.

I was finally able to produce the musical play I had written while living with Reverend Cameron. *Ebony and the Seven Dudes* was a black version of *Snow White and the Seven Dwarfs*. Rodney, who was a classmate of mine, had introduced me to his mom, and she had given me her typewriter so I could type my musical. She had told me that I could keep it if I promised to take good care of it. I secured backers to finance the costumes and props and found a junior high school that would allow me to use the auditorium. My father had high hopes that my production would take us from rags to riches (and I thought *I* was a big dreamer!), but this was an amateur play performed in a junior high school auditorium. It was great fun, and I'll always remember it, but it wasn't *Dreamgirls*.

That summer, while waiting to start at my new school, I signed up for a job as a counselor at a children's day camp. I enjoyed the job, but at the end of each day, I was exhausted. The best part of the job was going on field trips. I couldn't believe I was actually being paid to go out and have fun with those kids. On one of our trips to Jones Beach, a child's beach ball got away. It was already quite a distance from the shore by the time I saw it. Oblivious to any danger, I swam out to retrieve it. Several minutes later, I looked back at the shore, realized how far out in the ocean I was and panicked. I started swimming as hard as I could, but I tired quickly and started going under. In a few seconds, I had swallowed so much water that I thought I was going to die. A lifeguard saw me and, after a considerable struggle, managed to pull me safely to shore. Needless to say, I didn't come back with the beach ball, but I did come back with my life. I was so embarrassed that I wanted to quit the job, but with the encouragement of my supervisor and several coworkers, I managed to hang in there and finish the summer.

My father knew I'd made some extra money at the camp, and he wasn't shy about asking me for it. In fact, he started asking me for money with greater and greater frequency. At first I didn't mind, but after a while, I noticed that none of it was going to buy groceries. I didn't understand how a man could replace groceries with lavish clothing, drugs, and jewelry for his girlfriend. I made the mistake of sharing my frustration with my father's uncle Erby.

Uncle Erby drank a fifth of Scotch every day, but he had a nice car, a nice apartment, and a doting wife, so everybody respected him. I told him that I was the only one in the house working a legitimate job. Uncle Erby said he would talk to Dad. After talking with my father, Uncle Erby reported to me that Dad was really angry. He had told Uncle Erby that I was a liar, but Uncle Erby believed me. He gave me money to buy my own food and invited me to church with him that next Sunday. He suggested that I get involved in the youth fellowship at the church.

"There are some good kids you should get to know at Christ Temple, Shane. I think it will be good for you to meet them," he said.

I agreed to go with Uncle Erby to church the next Sunday. He went out and bought me a new suit and a white cashmere coat for the occasion. When I walked into the church, you couldn't tell me anything—I knew I was looking *good*! In addition, I really enjoyed the service. It was so different from a Catholic mass. The people were alive and friendly. Everyone, including Uncle Erby's family, was extremely nice to me.

Meanwhile, the situation with my father continued to spiral downward. His idea of good parenting was to give me a joint each morning before I left for school. In addition, the streets in his run-down neighborhood were becoming increasingly dangerous.

One day, I was standing in front of the apartment building when I saw my cousin Bucky, Uncle Erby's son, being chased down the street by several men. They pinned him against a van, took out a gun, put it to his head, and fired repeatedly, but the gun didn't go off. They continued to pull the trigger, and when they placed the gun at his side, it eventually fired. I ran upstairs to tell my father, but before Dad could get downstairs with his gun, the men who'd shot Bucky took off.

I'd heard that Bucky was on angel dust and that he was very close to losing his mind. The night before, I had seen him punch a man hard. The man had fallen to the pavement, hit his head, and later died. As if that were not enough trouble, the reason those men had been trying to kill Bucky was that he had told a pregnant woman that he was going to cut her baby out of her body. It was the father of that baby who had led the group that attacked and shot Bucky.

When my father and I got to him, Bucky was on the ground, bleeding badly from his gunshot wound. When the police and ambulance arrived, Bucky refused to go to the hospital. Afraid for Bucky's life, my father told the police about the man Bucky had assaulted the night before. Just as my father had planned, Bucky was taken off the streets and into custody where he would get the medical attention he needed. Besides, with those men trying to kill him, Dad thought that Bucky would be safer in jail than on the street. My father believed that he had done the right thing. Uncle Erby and Bucky did not agree. With Bucky in prison, Uncle Erby managed his pain and disappointment with a fifth of scotch and milk daily.

Nothing I had ever experienced in foster care could compare to what I was experiencing with my father. I knew that my life would go nowhere fast if I stayed with him. I was certain that, before long, he would have me selling drugs too. The last straw, however, was when I discovered that my father was part of a group that was stealing the identities of dead people in order to fraudulently collect their social security benefits. My father had assumed the identity of a James Patton. I can't begin to imagine the crimes he committed in Mr. Patton's name.

I was truly afraid of him by then. My father had a gun, and he wasn't even using his real name. He was violent and often threatened to hit me, but he never did—probably because of my seizures. His first wife had died of a seizure after one of their arguments, and I think he was afraid to hit me because of what had happened to her. Nevertheless, I was still afraid of him, and I began to plan my departure.

If I was going to escape without being caught, I knew I would have to outsmart one extremely nosy neighbor woman. She was always perched by her window where she could see, and ultimately report on, everything anybody did. I knew that if she saw me moving my things out, she would tell my father. To avoid suspicion, I took just a few things at a time.

One night I hailed a cab, not knowing exactly where I would go. I knew that I couldn't stay with anyone I had introduced my father to, because that would make it too easy for him to find me and because I didn't want to put anyone else in danger. Once again, the Moragnes came through for me by letting me store my things at their place. When I returned to my father's apartment that evening, he didn't suspect a thing.

My plan was to escape after school the next day. The next morning, I got ready for school as usual. My father gave me the customary breakfast joint and said, "See ya later, son"; out the door I went.

When the school day ended, it was time to make my getaway, but I didn't know where to go. Confused and scared, I went to Times Square to a place called Covenant House and signed myself in.

Looking at the bleak surroundings, all the mattresses on the floor, and the kids sleeping on them, I decided that I just couldn't stay there. Instead, I went to the police station across the street in the Port Authority terminal and turned myself in as a runaway from foster care. I shared my story of how I had grown up in foster care and had recently run away from a foster home to live with my father. I told the officer that I was running away from my father because I wanted to go back into foster care. I said that I had realized that running away from foster care was a big mistake and that I wanted another chance. The officer pulled up their records, but I was not listed as a missing person.

I'll be damned, I thought. The Catholic Home Bureau had never even reported me missing from the foster home they had placed me in. I wondered if they even cared that I had run away.

My father was notified, and before long, he and his girlfriend showed up at the police station. He told the officer that I was a pathological liar and that the whole story about being in foster care was made up. He swore to them that he had raised me and that I had a history of running away and lying. Obviously, he was very convincing, because the police released me into his custody.

As we drove back to Dad's place, I was terrified. He threatened me repeatedly.

"If I ever have to come to a police station again to get your ass, you won't live to regret it. Boy, I'll take you out."

At first, I just kept silent, but for some reason I made the mistake of responding to one of his threats.

"Why don't you just go ahead and do it then. Just do it!"

Suddenly, he slammed on the brakes, yanked me out, and slammed me against the car.

"What's wrong with you? You want me to whip your ass or something?"

I just stood there paralyzed. I didn't say a word for fear he would smack me or do something worse. Just in time, his girlfriend Joanne jumped out of the car to intervene.

"Shane, don't say anything. Just shut up. Don't say anything."

She was able to calm my father down, and we all got back into the car without anyone getting hurt. As we continued the drive home, I became more determined than ever to get away from him.

The next morning, I rushed to school to report my situation to my counselor. At about the same time, my father discovered that I had moved some of my things out of his apartment. His girlfriend noticed that most of my clothes were gone, and my father saw that my typewriter was missing, too. He immediately drove to school to find me.

He entered the hallway, yelling my name. I could hear him all the way down the hall in the counselor's office where I was hiding. The vice principal calmed him by threatening to call the police. After he left the building, my counselor snuck me out the back door and into a taxicab that took me to the Catholic Home Bureau.

During the ride, I wondered what I could possibly say to Mr. Pointer. Surely, he wouldn't be as eager to see me again as I would be to see him. Our last meeting hadn't gone particularly well. When I had been with the Edwards, Mr. Pointer had come to see me, and I had told him that I wasn't feeling the Edwards' home. He had shaken me and a tear had come down his face.

He had asked, "What are you doing? You have so much potential, and you are throwing away your life." He made me feel like I was actually impacting his life—that I mattered, that I wasn't just a case. I didn't say anything to him, and I didn't make any promises. I had been hurt so much by then that it was hard to believe that he really did care or that anyone did.

But on this visit, I tried to explain everything to Mr. Pointer. I told him that I had learned my lesson. I told him that I was horribly afraid of my father.

Then Mr. Pointer looked at me and asked, "What do you want us to do? We're afraid of your father too." He wanted to know why the bureau should take me back. Why should they put their lives at risk? "Why should we do this after all you've put us through?"

I had no answer. I cried and begged him to have them take me back, but he was unaffected by my tears. He said he wasn't going to let me manipulate the system anymore and that they weren't going to take me back. By then, I realized I was in big trouble. I had been exposed to life with my father, and I knew it was not the life I wanted to live.

Finally, it dawned on me to remind Mr. Pointer that I was still a ward of the state and that he and the agency were responsible for me until I was eighteen years old.

"I'm not leaving until you find me a home," I said.

Chapter 6
THE STORM IS OVER

In the midst of my battle, all hope was gone ...
I climbed the hills and saw the mountains,
I hollered help, because I was lost,
and then I felt a strong wind and a small voice saying,
"The storm is over."
—R. Kelly

The ultimatum I gave him worked. Mr. Pointer agreed to take me back into foster care. That same day, he found a place for me in a group home in Rego Park, Queens. Again, in search of something to ground and discipline me, I started attending Christ Temple Apostolic Church (Uncle Erby's church) every Sunday. The pastor's family often picked me up and brought me back to the group home, because they lived in Queens too.

On the way home from church one Sunday night, something that I can only describe as a miracle happened. A wintry mix of snow and sleet was falling while the pastor drove his wife, his two daughters, and me back to Queens. As we were crossing the Queensboro Bridge, the car started sliding and spinning out of control. Because of the heavy traffic on the bridge and the severity of the spin, we were almost certain to be hit by a car or to careen down a steep embankment. I just knew we were going to die.

The pastor tried desperately to get control of the car but with no success. We were still sliding and spinning from one side of the bridge to the other when the pastor's wife said, "In the name of Jesus." The moment she spoke those words, the car came to a complete stop, facing the embankment and clear of oncoming traffic. It was nothing short of a miracle. Only God could have enabled me to survive that danger and so many other life-threatening situations. That incident went a long way toward reinforcing my faith in God.

My brush with death caused me to take a closer look at my life and to take stock of where I was and where I was going. I was sixteen years old and had only two years left as a ward of the state. Confronting the reality of my situation, I decided that it was time to get it together. I'd said I wanted to get my life on track before, but I had greater urgency this time. I finally realized that I couldn't allow the pain and trouble I was experiencing to prevent me from achieving great things. It was time to move past the problems in my life and to focus on the opportunities that lay ahead. I needed to get myself ready for life after foster care. That meant getting serious about my education and planning a successful future.

When I moved to the Rego Park group home, I was enrolled in my fifth high school, John Bowne. When the school administrators looked at my credits and absenteeism rate, they predicted that I wouldn't graduate on time. That prediction was very discouraging, because I didn't want to be in the group home one day longer than I had to, and I wanted my high school diploma as soon as possible. However, things started looking up when I learned about Satellite Academy High, a unique school where I could complete independent study assignments that would help me make up the required credits for graduation. The school's principal assured me that I could do a lot of catching up, but he couldn't promise me that I would be able to graduate on time. I refused to be discouraged and looked forward to the challenge.

I started taking advantage of every opportunity I was offered. Nothing was going to deter me from graduating from high school. In addition to my regular classes, I did independent study and many other things to make up the classes I had missed because I had moved around so much. I took double loads so that I could graduate on time. In addition to independent course work, I participated in the cooperative work-study program. The program enabled me to put money in my pocket by affording me the opportunity to work for the Federal Aviation Administration (FAA) in the Noise Abatement Office. In addition to providing spending money, that job also helped me develop a strong work ethic and gave me another opportunity to chart my own destiny.

Because my days were structured in a way that captured my interests, I was able to focus and produce what was required of me, even with my ADD. I became the student government president, which tapped into what I had always been punished for before—my leadership skills. School wasn't frustrating anymore, and learning became exciting. I understood how we can each positively influence our atmospheres when we take control, and that made me hopeful.

With every success, my self-confidence grew, but success did have a downside. Sometimes, I got into fights when other residents of the group home called me "church boy" and "punk." They thought my goal-oriented attitude made me different, and it did.

I didn't have family to visit on weekends like most of the other teens in the group home, so I would sometimes spend weekends with my big brother Joe. It was always a treat when he picked me up in his sharp, navy blue Chrysler New Yorker and took me away from the group home for a while. Sometimes, while I was away on weekend visits or at church, the other kids would break into my room and steal things. Otherwise, my time away was enjoyable and very positive.

In spite of the conflicts that took place while I was at Rego Park, I did manage to make some good friends who seemed to be as motivated as I was to turn their lives around. One of those friends was Kenny, who, having grown up in an established white family, was sure that being in a group home with only black and Latino kids was nothing more than a bad dream. He was determined to get out of there as quickly as possible and to never look back. To make things easier on him, I agreed to become his roommate. He often referred to me as the only sane one in the group home. I told my roommate Kenny how great Satellite Academy High was and that I was very likely to make up my credits and graduate on time. After hearing me talk with such enthusiasm, Kenny enrolled as well.

In my homeroom class, there was a very attractive young lady named Tara. She was very slim with long, soft, bouncy hair. I was always a fool for women with pretty hair. We didn't connect right away, but that was okay, because I really wanted to hook up with the most popular girl in the school, Tracy. As luck would have it, Tracy asked me out, and I jumped at the opportunity. We hit it off right away, and things were going great; then suddenly, Tracy became as cold as ice toward me.

When I asked her what was up, I could hardly believe her response: "I just wanted to prove to the girls that I could get you if I wanted to," she boasted. "Mission accomplished." I had had no idea girls did that kind of stuff. She had no idea that she had broken my heart. I am pleased to say, however, that it was broken for only about a week—that's how long it took me to recover and start making moves toward Tara.

Tara lived in a group home that was within walking distance from mine, so one day, we walked home together. We began sneaking in and out of each other's group homes just to be together, and before long, she became my high school sweetheart.

In school, I discovered that I had the ability to lead and motivate people. I ran for president of the student government and won. Out of frustration with the quality of food and supervision at the group home, I created a newsletter called the *Rego Park Post*. I encouraged the other kids to submit poems or otherwise express their frustrations or observations. I typed the newsletter on my old typewriter and circulated it throughout the group home and to the foster care agency. To our amazement, the agency started listening and making the changes we wanted. We got results by channeling our energy productively. It was amazing.

Maybe it was this sense of empowerment that made me look at my time with Reverend Cameron in a different way. Although I could see the trials, I could also see his love for me, and I wrote him a letter telling him so and apologizing for all the problems I had caused him. He recently gave me a copy of that letter.

Dear Rev. Cameron

How are you doing? I gather you and your family are doing well. There are some things that I need to talk to you about. I would like to know what are your expectations of the letters to Keith that I would like to write. Whatever they are I will gladly respect them since you are his father.

Rev. Cameron I really want to apologize for the way I've behaved towards you and your family. As I look in my past, I see the many wrong things I've done to myself and other people around me. There are some things that I feel as a youngman I should correct if possible.

One of the major things that has really bothered my consience for a long time is the money that I owe to the people who thought so much of me and my production to sponsor it. That amount is $72.00 if I'm not mistaken, if I am please correct me.

Being I'm in the process of selling a percentage of Ebony And The Seven Dudes to a well known investor, I will receive some money shortly, therefore I'd like to pay that debut imediately. Please give me one more chance to straighten myself out. This is not just a bunch of words, I mean what I say. You see I'm now seeing Dr. Lewis once again because I realize that I do need medical attention, and I would like to correct myself before it's too late.

Rev. Cameron I realize what was my real reason for wanting so desperately to leave your home. I came to this conclusion with no one's help at all. As usual you were right, I was and I still am affraid of being loved. Another reason was that I was homesick for the big apple.

There is something I really want to tell you Rev. Cameron, No matter what I ever said to you, deep down in my heart I know that you are the best thing that ever happend to me since the Jenkins. You did all you could do for me and more, and I honestly love you very much for it. You've caused my life to take a real change of course. And as for your mother, well she's everything that these other homeless children wish for constantly. She's all that a grandmother should be.

I'd understand if you don't beleive me, and I know there's no way I can prove what I say in this letter is true.

```
              I am proud to let you know I am
now the Cheif Editor of this paper the Catholic
Home Bureau publishes called the Residents Post.
If you'd like I'll send you my first issue.

              Please write me back to let me know
how everyone feels about me at this point. It will
meomena alot to know I have true friends after all I've
done. Though I'm still trying to find out who I really
am, and what am I really all about. It will be very
reasureing to know your in my corner when the day
comes that I find the Shane that was meant to be.
```

Sincerly:

Shane L. Salter

Shane L. Salter

P.S Send my love to

Mammon

When I read it now, I am amazed at how quickly I was maturing at that time in my life.

As the year progressed, it finally became clear that I would graduate on time. I was extremely relieved that I had made it in spite of everything. At the senior awards assembly, I was stunned when it was announced that I was the valedictorian of my class. Could I possibly be the smartest person in the school? *How did this happen? I wasn't as competitive about grades as the other students.* A guy who had just wanted to graduate on time was graduating with honors, and I accepted the accolades with pride and dignity as Tara looked on. After attending six different high schools, three within my junior and senior years alone, I was graduating as valedictorian. The New York School of Printing, Julia Richman for the Performing Arts, St. Thomas Aquinas, Alfred E. Smith, and John Bowne were all fragments of my high school experience, but Satellite Academy was the place where I earned my diploma and the highest honor in the graduating class.

Tara and I went to the senior prom together. I wore a white tuxedo with tails. Tara was positively stunning in a lilac, custom-designed, satin gown and hat. We arrived in a white limousine, and when we walked in as the prom king and queen, everyone stopped and applauded. I felt as if I had been transformed from a frog into a prince and was living a storybook fairytale.

A whole new world was opening up for me, and the next step in my journey was college. I really needed some guidance on that subject, so I spoke with Dr. Lewis. She suggested that I pick a small college, because she thought I might find a large university overwhelming. I followed her advice, and every college I applied to accepted me. I couldn't believe so many doors were bursting wide open!

I called Mom Jenkins to give her the good news. I'd always stayed in touch with Mom Jenkins; I wanted her to know how much I missed her and loved her, and she was glad I still thought of her. She could hardly believe I was graduating, let alone as valedictorian. She agreed to come to the ceremony—in part, I suspect, because she thought I was lying, and she was going to have to see it for herself.

I called my grandmother to tell her about graduation and being named valedictorian. She was extremely proud of me. I asked if she would be willing to give me a special graduation gift, the telephone number of my great-grandmother, Flossy. I knew I was asking a lot, because Grandma and her mom, Flossy, did not get along at all. But it was important to me to try to have a relationship with my great-grandmother, and I wanted to invite her to my graduation. I was very grateful to Grandma for putting aside her differences long enough to give me the number. I called my great-grandmother right away, and Tara and I went to visit her.

My great-grandmother lived on the Upper West Side in Harlem. She had a beautiful apartment with imported French furniture and a baby grand player piano.

"Now I know where I get my taste. It must have skipped two generations or something," I joked.

We all had a good laugh. Then my great-grandmother talked about my mom, Sherry. Great-Grandma told me that she thought that Sherry's life would have turned out differently if she had been allowed to raise Sherry. Great-Grandma had wanted very much to raise my mother, but Grandma wouldn't let her. I wondered if that was why Great-Grandma Flossy and Grandma had been estranged for all those years. I wondered, *If things would have been different for Sherry, would I even be here?* I guess I'll never know.

Tara and I enjoyed our visit. I was very happy to have established a relationship with my great-grandmother, but there was still at least one more family rift I wanted to mend. I wanted to be reunited with my brother Keith, and I asked my new social worker, Ray, to help me. Ray wasn't sure he could help me get back together with Keith, but he was able to update me on what Keith had been up to since I'd last seen him. I was saddened to learn that Keith's adoption by Reverend Cameron had fallen through. After that, Keith had gone to Hillside Children's Center for a year and a half. Another couple, a Mr. and Mrs. Mills, took an interest in him and eventually adopted Keith. After the adoption, Mr. and Mrs. Mills got a stern warning from Reverend Cameron that I was a bad influence and that they had better keep Keith away from me.

I asked my social worker to ask the Mills if they would let me send a cassette tape that they could screen. Ray gave it a shot, and they agreed. After screening the tape, Mr. and Mrs. Mills concluded that I was anything other than a bad influence. In fact, they thought seeing me might help Keith, who was acting out. They decided to send him to New York City from Rochester, New York, to attend my graduation and to give us a chance to reconnect.

Graduation day finally came, and I was reunited with Keith.

"It's good to see you, big brother," he said, as we embraced one another. "I'm so proud of you."

It didn't matter what anyone else said or didn't say after that.

As I looked out over the audience when I delivered my valedictorian's speech, I saw my grandmother, my great-grandmother, Mrs. Jenkins, and Keith, and I felt as if the fibers of my life were coming back together.

My grandmother started bragging about how proud she was until my great-grandmother told her, "Be quiet. The only one deserving of any credit for that boy is his mother, Mrs. Jenkins."

I agreed with great-grandmother in principle, but it really was something for us all to celebrate as a family, regardless of our history and our pain. It seemed like the celebration had barely started when it was time for Keith to go back to Rochester. I promised to stay in touch and told him I would visit him. In fact, I decided to attend Elmira College, which was only a couple of hours away from Rochester, just to be closer to him. I wanted to try to be what I hadn't been able to be for him when I was younger—a role model. I wanted to encourage him to hold on, to believe in his dreams, and to know that tomorrow would be better than today. I also hoped he would understand that I had never meant to hurt him. I had only wanted to protect him

Immediately after high school graduation, I worked three jobs to earn money for school. I was a file clerk at the Social Security Administration on weekdays, I served as a front desk clerk at a Best Western Hotel on weeknights, and I worked at a nightclub called Justine's on weekends.

Later that summer, I found out that Tara was pregnant. I begged her to keep our baby, but she wouldn't. Even Tara's group home director advised her to have an abortion and tried to discourage me from pursuing a romantic relationship with Tara.

"You will eventually outgrow her, Shane," the director predicted.

I couldn't believe that a nun was saying this and that she was encouraging Tara to have an abortion. I told Tara that I was willing to forgo Elmira College and attend Hunter College, which was closer to her, so she, our baby, and I could be a family. I said I would do whatever was required to ensure that she and our child had everything they needed. My mother had spared my life when she had had the opportunity to abort me under very similar circumstances. And, because she didn't, I was alive. While I had not had the best life, I was hopeful and believed in a future filled with promise for myself and for the next generation.

I thought I had her convinced to keep the baby. But while I was working at the hotel one night, she called to inform me that she was on her way to have an abortion and that there was nothing I could do to change her mind. When Tara decided that it was in her best interests to abort our child, it felt as if she killed a part of me. I could only imagine what our little boy might have looked like. On that night, I vowed never to have anything to do with Tara again.

The day finally came when I left the Rego Park group home and became a freshman at Elmira College in upstate New York. I was determined to major in anything but social work, and I ultimately decided on health and human services. Maybe subconsciously I had made the decision to be a health care major because Ma Jenkins had gone back to school to become a registered nurse. Things went great that first semester. New York State covered my room and board, and my tuition was covered by Pell Grants, student loans, and by a partial scholarship from Elmira. I was enjoying myself and doing well in classes.

But as I was preparing to go home for the Christmas break, I realized something: I had no home to go back to. All my college friends were making plans to go home to spend time with their families. Meanwhile, the group home had given away my room to a new resident. The staff did, however, offer me the option of sleeping on their couch. The situation was a painful reminder that abused and neglected children who overcome tremendous challenges and manage, against all odds, to survive the foster care system, still end up without a home. It didn't seem right for them and it certainly didn't feel right for me. I concluded that there was something very wrong with the system.

It was a great comfort when Mr. and Mrs. Mills, who had adopted my brother Keith, invited me for Christmas. The Mills were excited when they learned about the discipline I had acquired to overcome the challenge of living on campus without any support. Because they valued education, they laid out the welcome mat, and I jumped at the opportunity. Being welcomed into their family was the greatest Christmas gift I could have received. I started staying with the Mills family during every holiday, and it was such a relief to have a place to call home again. Gradually, the sick feeling I got every semester break when friends would start talking about their families began subsiding. And after I had explained how disheartening it was not to receive mail at school, Ma Mills even started sending me care packages.

I didn't bother to explain to my classmates that I had been a foster child. I just claimed Mom and Dad Mills as my parents too. It felt good to say that my dad was an associate professor at SUNY Brockport and that my mom was the minority business enterprise officer for the city of Rochester. I eventually realized that I needed to learn to drive, so Dad Mills taught me in his Chevy Malibu. It felt great to do something sons normally do with their fathers.

But calling someone Mom and Dad and being able to truly count on them when trouble comes are two different things. One night I was returning from a trip to New York City, when my car broke down in the mountains of upstate New York. It was so late and I was still so far from Rochester that I didn't feel I could call the Mills family. There was no one else for me to contact. I was fortunate to get help from a stranger who put me up for the night, paid for my ruined tire, and sent me on my way the next morning. I shudder to think what might have happened if I hadn't been so lucky.

College life continued to go well. I stayed at Elmira College for the first two years; then I applied to Morehouse College and was accepted. However, some unexpected news threatened to derail my train.

Tara had visited Elmira a few months previously in an attempt for us to get back together, but it hadn't worked out. Unfortunately, that visit had resulted in another pregnancy. She was three months along, and this time, I was determined that she wasn't going to have an abortion.

The situation was further complicated by the fact that, since things were supposedly over between Tara and me, I had fallen madly in love with Janice, a fellow Elmira student. Janice was not only one of the prettiest young ladies on campus, but she was also one of the smartest. Janice's first reaction to the pregnancy news was that we would survive it. She understood my foster care history and knew how much I'd want to be there for my kid. But being a dad from a distance was not acceptable to me. I told Janice that we had to end our relationship so that Tara and I could have a chance for the baby's sake. Janice said she understood, and we said our good-byes.

If getting pregnant was Tara's way of getting us back together, it worked. Because of her and the baby, I decided not to go to Morehouse.

My big brother Joe was outraged. He told me that I'd be throwing my life away if I didn't insist that Tara abort the baby. I didn't agree. I could not sanction aborting my child, because every time I looked in the mirror, I was reminded of how close my mother had come to aborting me. I also remembered God's intervention on my behalf. Instead, I enlisted in the Navy's BOOST program, which would eventually make me a commissioned officer. This enlistment was my way of ensuring that our baby would not have to go through the things I had gone through. Joining the service allowed me to provide for my wife and child and to finish my education at the same time.

I was scheduled to leave for the Navy's BOOST program on June 28, but the baby was due between June 28 and July 5. Although I wanted to be present for the delivery, securing my family's future seemed more important. Tara didn't agree. She wanted me there when she gave birth, so I met with my recruiter and forfeited my slot in

BOOST and my opportunity to obtain a commission. After I received my associate's degree on June 5 from Elmira College, Tara and I left for New York City.

My old Volkswagen had worn-out shock absorbers, and the bumpy ride back to New York might have caused Tara to go into labor. In any case, on June 8, three to four weeks before she was due, Tiffany Monique Salter was born at about twelve thirty am. Tara and I were both nineteen. Tiffany was born crying and shivering, but when the nurse placed her in my arms, the shivering and crying stopped. As a tear fell from my eye, I looked into hers and promised her that she would never know the pain I had known. Everything I did from that day forward was for my precious baby girl.

After Tiffany was born, Tara went to live in a teen mom and baby program. My departure date for the navy had become September 23. Before I left for the navy, we were secretly married. I wanted to be sure that Tiffany never felt illegitimate if I lost my life in combat.

Meanwhile, I quickly took the best-paying job I could find in New York City, which was in the housekeeping department of a Jewish nursing home. As a union member, I was actually making more money mopping, waxing, and buffing floors than many of the administrative assistants earned. I wore a gray housekeeping uniform, which I found humbling, because I had just graduated from college.

People in the building usually didn't speak to me when I wore that uniform. When they turned up their noses, I would mumble under my breath, "I probably make more money than you anyway." Because of the terrible way I was treated, I made a promise that I would never look down on anyone because of that person's job. I worked as many hours as they would give me, just to be sure that Tiffany and Tara were well taken care of.

When September 23 came, I left for boot camp in San Diego, California, as planned. Just a few weeks into boot camp, Tara wrote to me, saying, "I'm tired of you being away. If this is the way our life is going to be, then I want a divorce." What was I to do? I didn't want to be in boot camp, getting my butt whipped in the blazing heat. I was there only because I had a family that needed instant income security. It was our ticket out of the foster care system for certain.

How could she send me that kind of letter? *Damn, how dare she?* I thought. *Here I go again. Not in my adult life, too! Right out of the gate,*

I'm trying to create my own family, and she's ready to walk out on me just like everyone else. I wanted to throw in the towel right there and say, "Forget it." I asked myself what the fight was really for and how much more I would have to put up with. I wondered if anyone ever hung in there with anyone else for the long haul, and I almost started feeling sorry for myself. Then I looked at a picture of Tiffany, and suddenly, everything was all right. The struggle was for Tiffany, my baby girl, so she would not have to pay for the sins of her parents the rest of her life.

I wrote back to Tara and told her never to send me a letter like that again. I reminded her that I was getting my ass kicked in boot camp for her and Tiffany and that I didn't need that kind of distraction. Later, I learned that that letter was Tara's way of letting me know she was having an affair. I believe her affair resulted in her third pregnancy, even though she claimed I was the father. Apparently, Tara found out she was pregnant again a few weeks after I left for boot camp, and for the second time, she had an abortion. We remained together, because I was focused on the baby I had just left behind.

I was determined to complete boot camp and become a hospital corpsman. That experience would enable me to provide for my family and to ultimately become a hospital administrator. To reach my goal, I had to reenroll in college immediately after boot camp. I could see myself running a clinic, overseeing a department within a medical facility, or maybe even serving as the CEO of a hospital somewhere. I had big dreams, and I had a plan. But my plan was seriously threatened when I couldn't pass my swim test.

After failing for the fourth time, I wrote to Tara and said, "I may not make it. They are threatening to kick me out if I don't pass the next time. If they do, I guess I'll try the Air Force." Thank God, I passed the next time, and my Navy career was back on track.

I had been proud when I graduated from high school as valedictorian, but that was nothing compared to the pride I felt when I graduated from boot camp. As we marched and the band played the national anthem, I got chills up my spine. I had officially become one of America's own. I finally belonged somewhere. I had an identity as a sailor in the United States Navy.

After graduating, I remained in San Diego for the rest of the year and completed requirements to become a hospital corpsman. I was asked to list the top places I wanted to be stationed. My first choice was Charleston, South Carolina, because I had heard it was a big navy town, which would be a lot of fun. It also wasn't too far from Tara's mother on Hilton Head. My second choice was the National Naval Medical Center in Bethesda, Maryland, because I was told that was where the big brass was, and if I were noticed there, it could really propel my career. I ended up in Bethesda. I was very eager to start family life, so I found an apartment right away. Tara and Tiffany arrived a couple of weeks later. I was so proud. I even invited Mrs. Jenkins and Robby down to show off our new apartment. Much to my surprise, they actually came.

While stationed there, I completed my rotation on the inpatient wards, working deadly, rotating shifts. I did so well that, in record time, I petitioned to be assigned to a clinic so I could go back to school. My petition was honored, and I was assigned for the next few years to the Pediatric Acute Care Clinic. I enrolled in the base's external degree program through Southern Illinois University at Carbondale, majoring in health care management. Eventually, I became the senior corpsman in the clinic, and my superiors strongly encouraged me to enroll in the Armed Forces Medical School to become a physician. My commander, who was impressed with my ambition and clinical skills, said that if I wanted it, he would make it happen.

Well, I knew I did not want to be a physician badly enough to endure all that I would have to endure to get there. Second, I knew that Tara's support was weak, at best.

Tara resented the amount of time I spent on my studies. We were about twenty years old, and Tara felt we should be clubbing more and having an active social life. I promised her that socializing would come in time, and I tried to convince her that my education was an investment in our future. She was obviously not very committed to our marriage. Shortly after being assigned to the pediatric clinic and relocating Tara and Tiffany from New York, I had found an unmailed love letter that she had written to another man. As much as I wanted to create my own family, my ego could not handle the affair, and I asked for a divorce. It was ugly. We fought and fought for a long time before agreeing to go our separate ways.

Initially, we agreed that I would have custody of Tiffany. Then Tara suddenly changed her mind, and I was devastated. She figured she could get money from me if she took Tiffany with her. To further complicate our impending separation, Tara was pregnant again. Despite my objections, Tara decided to have another abortion.

"I'll have a better chance of finding someone with one child than with two," she said.

At that point, for the first time, I was so angry with her that I actually wanted her to have an abortion. I even gave her the money for it. I was, however, quite devastated to learn later that we had aborted twins.

The day Tara left with my baby girl, my world shattered. I refused to fight for custody, because I didn't want to establish a precedent for her to use Tiffany as a way to get at me. To add salt to the wound, Tara decided that they would move to Hilton Head, South Carolina, to live with Tara's mother. She knew how much I loved Tiffany. Why would she move so far away? Why wouldn't she just go back to New York, a place I could get to in four hours?

Shortly after Tara left, I moved into a townhouse with two roommates. One weekend, I planned a drive to New York to visit Joe and to show him my new car. I called a couple of nights before to confirm that I was coming, but I got no answer. I found that odd, because, as a senior employee at Western Electric, he had instant access to the latest technological equipment. Surely he, at least, had an answering machine. After not being able to get in touch with him, I decided to postpone the trip until I could be sure that Joe was in town.

The next Tuesday, the Red Cross summoned me. When I arrived at the Red Cross offices, they told me that Joe had been robbed and killed in New York. I had another reason to hate New York City. My head was still spinning as I learned that Joe was going to be buried the next day. I booked the first flight available, but it was delayed, and I missed the funeral. A friend picked me up at the airport and rushed me to the cemetery. Joe's casket had already been laid in the ground. I never had the chance to see him again or to say good-bye to him.

The pain was even deeper than it had been when I had learned of my mother's death. I was devastated. My big brother, mentor, friend, and confidant was gone. I made my way to where the family had gathered after Joe's funeral and spoke with a friend of Joe's, who told me that I should never try to find a replacement for Joe in my life, because there never would be one. That was the best advice he could have given me. No one understood me like Joe had, no one motivated me like Joe had, and no one loved me like Joe had. Every day of my life, I still miss him. He was my hero. I wish he could see the man I've become. He'd be pleased to know that I hung in there in spite of it all.

A year later, my ex-wife called and said that she could no longer provide for Tiffany and asked me to take permanent custody. What was I supposed to do? I was living with two other guys in a three-bedroom townhouse in Silver Spring, Maryland, but I couldn't let that stand in the way. Somehow, I worked it out with Zarick and Jesse to have Tiffany come live with us for a while. Tiffany and I would share the same room at first, but shortly after she arrived, Zarick moved out, and Tiffany got her own room.

Tiffany was two years old when I got custody of her. Even as a single parent, I was determined that she would have the life of a princess. She went with me everywhere. Eventually, Tiffany and I were able to get our own place in Rockville, Maryland. To finish my degree and earn additional income, I had female friends watch Tiffany in shifts. I was enrolled in school full-time, was working part-time, and was fulfilling my last year in the navy.

After I completed my four years in the navy, I didn't reenlist. On the day of my discharge, I stood in front of the National Naval Medical Center with Tiffany beside me.

"Here in Maryland is where we will plant our roots," I vowed. "We will redefine what it means to be a Salter."

I decided that I would transition from navy active duty to air force reserve. Now, to many people that didn't make much sense, because the navy and the air force are not at all similar, but the difference made it more exciting for me. I had always been intrigued by the air force. I was offered a position as an entry-level supervisor at Children's Hospital in Washington DC, and I joined the air force reserve.

My air force experience only confirmed how much more I liked the navy, and I privately questioned the logic of my decision to join the air force—until I met a sweet, unassuming young lady. She had a radiant smile and never had a strand of hair out of place. As far as substance goes, she was the most solid woman I'd ever met. At first, I wasn't interested in her romantically—I didn't think she was my type—but I certainly wanted her to be my friend.

After promising month after month to call her, I ran into her and struck up a conversation about a challenge I was facing. Tiffany was about to be christened. The sleeves on her beautiful, white, christening dress were too long, and I didn't know how to sew. Gloria agreed to take the dress home and alter it for me. After the christening, I invited her over for dinner with Tiffany and me as a gesture of gratitude. That was the night I discovered that Gloria had been adopted, which explained why I felt connected to her. There were no fireworks between us, but because she had been adopted, I somehow knew that she could identify with me on a level most people couldn't.

Chapter 7
I WILL STAY WITH YOU

I will stay with you,
Through the ups and the downs,
I will stay with you,
When no one else is around.
When the dark clouds arise,
I will stay by your side.
—John Legend and Dave Tozer

Gloria and I became good friends, and then one day, I realized that I was romantically attracted to her. Something changed for me when she tried to hook me up with a friend of hers who was not even in Gloria's league. Right after that setup, I expressed my interest in Gloria, and we started dating. I was having a really hard time getting up the nerve for the first kiss.

Then my friend Harold told me, "You had better kiss that woman before she thinks something is wrong with you." The pressure was on. When I finally kissed Gloria, we were standing by the car one night, saying good-bye after a date while Tiffany waited in the backseat. Tiffany was so excited that she called her "Mommy." That's when Gloria did something that truly impressed me. She said to Tiffany, "I'm not your mother, sweetie," and gave her a hug. She took an awkward situation and handled it directly yet with great sensitivity.

After that first kiss, I knew I wanted to marry Gloria, but I hadn't filed for divorce from Tara. I had told Tara that if she wanted a divorce, she was going to pay for it. I didn't have much money, and what I did have was for Tiffany. I had told Tara to just file, and I wouldn't contest it. After taking such a stance, I knew if I sent her divorce papers, she would know something was up and become obstructive just for the hell of it. Gloria made it clear to me that I shouldn't even think about proposing to her until my divorce was final. Well, under the circumstances, I thought I might have to wait for years.

Then a few weeks later, a miracle happened. Unsolicited, divorce papers arrived from an attorney in South Carolina, who was representing Tara. I took the arrival of those papers as a sign. Gloria was the woman for me, and she was the stepmother Tiffany deserved.

Right away, I started preparing to purchase a ring, and again Gloria dropped a gentle hint. "If you need help paying for it, let me know," she said. I interpreted that as code for, "Don't bring me a diamond chip: nothing less than a half-karat will do."

I couldn't stop laughing, but I also got the message. I found a great ring, I proposed, and Gloria accepted.

Meanwhile, my little brother Keith had been living with me for almost a year. Keith said his plan was to go into the service, but I don't think those were ever his true intentions. I leveraged my reputation and relationships to get him a job at Children's Hospital, only to see him terminated within the first month. Fortunately, not many people knew he was my brother, and the embarrassment was minimal.

Keith took every opportunity to remind me of the pain he had endured after I had left him behind in Rochester.

"Enough already," I remember saying. "How many times are we going to talk about this?" I repeatedly tried to explain that I had made the best decision I could under the circumstances. "For crying out loud, I was fifteen!" I shouted.

That underlying issue remains unresolved for him to this day. Every conversation between the two of us circles back to when I left him behind at the age of twelve in Rochester.

One time, the tension between us escalated to a fistfight in my apartment. A few inches taller than me, he thought he could whip me, but I was determined to show him otherwise. Our relationship should never have deteriorated to a physical confrontation, but when it did, our rage was intense, and I was afraid that future fights might lead to the death of one of us. Because witnessing such violent encounters could be detrimental to five-year-old Tiffany, I asked Keith to leave.

Keith moved to Washington DC, angry with me and very uncertain about where he belonged. He resolved to survive by any means necessary. I heard from him from time to time, but our relationship became increasingly strained. It was challenging, but we never lost sight of the fact that we were brothers and loved each other very much. Therefore, when Keith called in need of a place to stay, I offered my apartment. It was getting close to my wedding day, so Tiffany and I were spending most of our time at Gloria's anyway. I gave Keith my apartment, fully furnished, with the understanding that he would pay the utilities. Keith was elated, and I was glad that I could do something to help him, but it turned out to be a big mistake.

I went by the apartment one day to pack some of my things and was shocked to find it filthy. The electricity hadn't been paid, the lights had been turned off, and the refrigerator was completely defrosted. As if that were not enough, I walked into Tiffany's room to find her ceramic piggy bank shattered and all of the money we had been saving since her birth gone. At that moment, my heart was shattered too. He couldn't have hurt me more if he had tried.

I couldn't find Keith for weeks, but he resurfaced just before the wedding. Originally, he was supposed to be a groomsman, but I did not want to rely on him for a role that wasn't easily replaceable, so I asked him to perform the less demanding task of escorting distinguished guests down the aisle. He was supportive and agreed. Meanwhile, Gloria and I had already started shopping for a house. We found a beautiful home in Fort Washington, Maryland, on almost two acres of land, and we were able to move in a few months before the wedding.

Then, the day arrived for me to marry the woman who had become my best friend. Ebenezer AME Church in Fort Washington, Maryland, was beautifully decorated for the occasion. Keith escorted Gloria's adoptive mother down the aisle. Despite several knee surgeries and having to use a walker, she was determined to make that walk. Representing me were three sets of parents: Mom and Dad Mills, Mom and Dad Moragne, and Mom Jenkins. Pop Jenkins was not able to make it, but Robbie Jenkins was there. My grandmother was there too, beaming with pride along with my mother's baby brother, Uncle Pierre.

My mom's sister, Jewel, who was the latest family casualty of drug addiction, used the occasion to create a scene. She demanded a rose and insisted on someone escorting her down the aisle like an official member of the bridal party. I'm sure the entire church could hear her yelling in the vestibule, "I am his dead mother's sister and I should be given her props." Jewel refused to be quiet until one of the hostesses took the rose off her garment and pinned it on Jewel's dress. Then Keith escorted her down the aisle.

With all the drama behind us, I was finally, after so many years, going to have the family I had always dreamed of. Attired in his air force dress blues, Technical Sergeant Douglas Bell almost stole the show as he rolled out the red carpet in cadence. The sight of my sister, Shanique, who was a junior bridesmaid, and Tiffany, who was the flower girl, brought tears to my eyes.

Those initial tears were just the beginning of my emotions, however, because when Gloria walked in, no one came close to her radiance. For the first time, nothing about my past mattered, because our future was so bright. I was on my way to building the family that had existed, until then, only in my dreams.

A year later, our first child together, Brittney Nicole, was born. Gloria and I learned in advance that we were having a girl, and while I had tried not to let it show, that time I had really hoped for a boy. After sixteen hours of labor, the baby's heart rate was dropping, and the doctor decided to perform an emergency caesarean section. When Brittney emerged, she was blue and not breathing. At that moment, I thought I was being punished for wanting a boy instead of just being thankful for a healthy baby. I prayed to God to save our baby and spare my wife.

"She doesn't deserve this. Please save our baby," I pleaded.

Within minutes, Brittney was breathing.

After our second daughter, Courtney Shanade, was born a few years later, we decided that if we were going to have sons, they would be adopted.

Our first son, Rico Giovanni, came to us at the age of six. Rico was biracial, too dark for white families, and considered undesirable by most black families. The combination of his race and his age classified him as hard to place. However, he was anything but undesirable to Gloria and me. We couldn't wait to see him.

Our first meeting was thrilling, and I couldn't get over the fact that he looked so much like me. The agency told me that although he had been diagnosed with separation anxiety as a preschooler, he had responded well to treatment and was a well-adjusted kid. He was wearing checkered pants and a striped shirt with a coat full of dirt and grease. We wondered what kind of foster home would send a child to meet prospective parents dressed like that. Perhaps one with a strategic agenda. If the child looked pathetic, the prospective parents might feel overwhelmed with sympathy and move quickly to get him out of there. Gloria and I instantly decided that he would join our family.

During his first preplacement weekend visit with us, Rico's responses to questions seemed programmed. For example, if I asked him why he was doing something he shouldn't have been doing, his response was "Because I'm bad." It became clear that these obviously programmed responses were meaningless to him. I also noticed that he sometimes struggled to understand questions. I wondered if he was hard of hearing.

Gloria and I met with Rico's teachers, hoping they could shed some light on his behavior. The teacher we spoke to showed us Rico's consistent A and B coursework. She knew him well and was certain that all he needed was to be adopted.

"Please give him a home. He is so sweet. He just needs a good home," she said.

My heart ached for him, just as my heart had ached when I was in Rico's shoes as a little boy, hoping that someone would give me a home. He was brought to the classroom that day dressed in purple, corduroy pants that seemed to be about two sizes too small. All I could think about was getting him some new clothes and trashing those tight, purple pants. He must have been humiliated, dressed like that. Later that day, we met his foster parents, who reminded me of the Balfours. Just like the Balfours, Rico's foster mother did not intend to adopt him, but they had adopted a little girl who had came into their home after Rico. An original plan to reunite Rico with his birth father hadn't worked out, and that event had cleared the way for us to become his family.

Rico had been in foster care since the age of one. His father was an alcoholic, and his mother suffered from schizophrenia. We were told that he was predisposed, but we didn't know that sons of schizophrenic mothers were at higher risk than daughters. Truthfully, I don't think it would have made a difference in our decision. We thought it was possible he would become schizophrenic, not probable, and we never watched for it or thought about it again.

Rico made it clear that he didn't like his name and wanted to be named after me. I couldn't have been prouder, and I could certainly understand why he associated belonging and security with his name. However, I told him that one of the few things he had received from his birth mother was his name and that I thought he should keep part of it. Therefore, he became Shane Lenard Rico Salter Jr., and I added Rico to my name to become Shane Lenard Rico Salter Sr.

Shortly after he came to us, I noticed he was having difficulties in school. At first, I figured the problems had arisen because he was still adjusting to life with us. However, when things didn't seem to get any better, I made an appointment with the Department of Psychiatry and Speech Pathology at Children's Hospital, where I worked as a hospital administrator. The psychologist gave us several diagnoses, but Shane Rico's major problem was receptive language disorder, which is similar to dyslexia. Gloria and I addressed his needs through special education services and in-home therapy. The following year, Shane Rico's adoption became final.

Shane Rico also had trouble controlling his anger. From the start, we went to great lengths to reassure him that we were his family and that we were never going to give up on him, no matter how many problems he had. The more we reassured him that he was loved and this home was it, the easier it was for him to let go of the hurt and anger that had built up, but we still had too many busted walls and windows to count over the years. I found it interesting that Shane Rico would do most of his damage when I wasn't in the house. Tiffany would always say, "Dad, he acts very differently when you're not home."

He was a challenging child from the beginning, but he was my first son, so I thought he was different from the girls just because he had more testosterone. I rather naïvely tried to write his behavior off as normal. I believed that he behaved differently around me and always wanted to be with me, because he felt that I was the only one who understood him. I'd been in his shoes before, and I did everything I could to let him know I accepted him unconditionally. He had also never had a man in his life. I think that, having lived in a foster home with sisters and a foster mom who wouldn't adopt him after six years, he was guarded against gestures of love and commitment from women, and he never deeply bonded with his new mom and sisters, although he enjoyed them.

Shane Rico was focused, serious, and intense. I noticed he didn't enjoy the things other children his age enjoyed. He didn't like to play with groups of other children, but he liked being with one friend at a time. Again, I identified with him. When I was a child, the nuns in Catholic school had always punished me for my difficulties with social behavior, and I remember how great it had felt just sitting with Dad Jenkins, watching *60 Minutes*, instead of trying to play with other kids and toys. I had always been a loner, intense, and serious. Unlike Shane Rico, I was able to develop a superficial extraverted personality to survive, but it had nothing to do with whom I really was.

Shane Rico and I looked forward to special moments while we were driving. He would ask me questions about everything, and we'd sing our favorite song "All by myself, don't want to be all by myself any more ..." We would sing that song on the way to the store, on the way to school, and even when we went fishing. We always sang. He would crack up, watching me act out some of the lyrics to other songs. Each time, I'd say, "Hold on, that's my favorite song."

One day, Shane Rico busted me; he said, "Dad, they're all your favorite songs."

I guess he was right. I love music, and so does he.

On one occasion as we were crossing a bridge in the car, he jumped with excitement at the beauty and magnitude of the open body of water. He just took it all in and enjoyed the moment. Even though he struggled, he was capable of great joy.

As much as Shane Rico and I got along, unfortunately, the holes in our walls were getting larger with each new outburst, and I started to realize that Shane Rico was having more than just a little trouble handling his anger. His tantrums grew more frequent, and he started getting angry for no reason—for example, if somebody just looked at him wrong. The other children in the family started warning me, saying, "You should see the way he looks at Mom sometimes when you're gone; he looks at her like he's gonna snap when she tells him to do something."

I thought back to my anger and rage when I was a kid, but I couldn't identify with this. His behavior seemed extreme at times—especially the day when he was confronted about something he did and reacted by flying off to his room and putting his fist through the window. He was ten years old at the time.

"Have you lost your mind?" I asked him.

Shortly afterwards, we had to hospitalize him for depression. He was flat, didn't want to play, and didn't respond to anything. My concern grew deeper when, one night, Gloria did a bed check, and he wasn't there. She searched the house and finally found him playing with candles. He had put all of our lives in jeopardy. We looked at each other and declared we needed help. We called a meeting at school and got him a new Individualized Education Plan (IEP), which called for intensive psychological support services in the classroom and a smaller class size. Through Prince George's County, we received in-home counseling as well, but not much progress was made.

One blessing during this trying time in our life was the relationship I developed with my grandmother. We'd begun talking on the phone regularly, and I was trying to appreciate our relationship for everything it was becoming, rather than grieving for all that it had not been. Over time, each telephone conversation ended with my asking her when she was going to leave New York and come spend some time with me. Each time, she'd give me the same answer, "Oh, it won't be long." One day, however, when I called and she gave me that usual answer, I wouldn't accept it.

I said, "Ma, all of these years, I've never needed nor asked anything from you, but I need you now. I need you to come down and be with me. Let me lie in your lap like a baby, and just hold me. I also need you to get to know my kids and for them to get to know you."

Not a second passed before she said, "I'll be there."

She came, and I did just as I'd told her I needed to do. After a couple of days, I put my head in her lap and just lay there. She caressed my face. As I told her how tired I was, tears started to fall.

"I don't know how much more of this I can do. I've been fighting all my life to survive, trying not to repeat the mistakes of my mom and dad. But every day, it seems to get harder. It's a struggle getting through. Sometimes I'm tired of carrying this burden and of feeling as if nobody understands how hard it is to be me."

"I know, baby, I know," she said softly. And I just lay there quietly. For the first time since my mom had walked out on me, I was being held and touched by a parent. It was a strange sensation, and it let me know that I was human.

I never had to ask again. Grandma's visits became steady. My home was her second home, her escape from New York.

She began to change—to soften and open up—as we spent time together. We both did. I laughed with her and teased her about her weight, and she teased me about mine. It's somewhat funny that everything I hoped to find in all those homes, I ultimately found with my grandmother, a woman who had at first rejected me. I often wonder what my life would have been like if I'd just left her alone, not pursued her. I would never have experienced the beauty and strength of our relationship, and neither would my children have.

Little did I know how much I would need her in the days and years to come.

Chapter 8

NEVER GIVE UP

If something inside
Keeps inspiring you to try,
Don't stop, and never give up.
Don't ever give up on you.
—Yolanda Adams

Watching my grandmother and my children interact felt great, although at times, it felt unbelievable to the point of fantasy. Grandma didn't miss anything. I don't know why, but something inside me warmed up when I heard her scold them. Perhaps it was the knowledge that my wife had someone she could consistently rely on for relief from all the kids. Maybe it was hearing my children call her "Grandma" and knowing that they were experiencing what I had never had. Whatever it was, it made me feel as if I belonged somewhere, even if I got there through my children.

It's amazing what can happen when you work hard at forgiving, letting go, and living in the present. The love I wasn't able to get from a family as a child, I got as a man through my children, wife, and grandmother.

At times, Grandma and I were inseparable, and then at times when my moods kicked in, I felt claustrophobic, as if I were suffocating. Those moments passed quickly, though. One thing was for sure—Shane loved his grandma, and Grandma sure loved her grandson Shane.

Given our history, not many people understood how our relationship had evolved into something this great. Some immediate and extended family members even resented that I dropped everything when she called and that every need she had, that I was aware of, was attended to. You could say, "Time heals wounds," but that would be too trite. I prefer the Covey principle, "Seek first to understand, before seeking to be understood." I try to live by that principle in all that I do. When I have turned away from something or someone, it is either because I have exhausted my capacity for understanding or because I found malice in the heart of the person or in that person's intent.

Though my growing relationship with my grandmother was a great joy in my life, there were still many great struggles. We were still trying to help Shane Rico in his battle with his anger and depression, and Gloria and I were also trying to help other members of my family as much as we were able.

In the middle of Shane Rico's drama, my brother Keith came to stay with us in exchange for helping around the house and watching the children. I then received a call that my other brother, my father's son David, had been arrested in New York. Two years earlier, I had driven up for David's junior high school graduation when he was fourteen. At that time, I had tried everything to convince his grandmother to let him move in with me. I had been troubled by the crowd he was associating with and by his defeatist attitude. Someone had asked him after graduation where his father was, and I had quietly watched as David said, "He's dead."

I asked him why he had said that, and he said, "You could come all the way from Maryland, Shane, but our so-called father couldn't come from Harlem up to the Bronx for my graduation."

Dad's absence hurt David deeply. Each promise our father made and didn't keep had taken a toll. David was becoming increasingly sad, hopeless, and filled with rage. His capacity to dream of life beyond the projects of Mott Haven was diminished by the countless number of hardened friends he associated with. I told his grandmother, Ms. Jones, that it was time for him to be around a consistent, positive, male role model, but she refused to let him live with me. She needed him to help with his two other sisters and his cousin, who were also being raised in her two-bedroom apartment.

Now, David was sixteen and had already been arrested. He was almost certainly on his way to Rikers Island.

We were at a crossroads. David was no longer listening to his grandmother. He was coming and going as he pleased, and he was facing jail time. I went to New York to speak to the judge on his behalf. I promised the court that New York would never have a problem with David again if the judge would allow me the chance to intervene. I asked him to release David into my custody and to let him move with me to Maryland. The judge said yes, and finally, David's grandmother agreed to let him live with my family.

Soon after David's arrival, Gloria and I learned that he drank very heavily almost every day. Such behavior was, of course, unacceptable. David was not allowed to drink Monday through Friday. He didn't stop, but we were able to modify his drinking. We enrolled him in a GED program. We also monitored his every movement, which prompted him to call his grandmother and tell her that he thought I hated him. However, unlike my brother Keith, David responded to my attempts to get him on track. We agreed that he would not work, because we wanted his focus to be on getting his diploma. That agreement made him miserable, but it paid off. David passed his GED on his first attempt.

After he got his GED, I got David a job at Children's Hospital. He promised that he would not repeat Keith's mistake and put me in the position of having to explain his misconduct. He kept his promise. I heard nothing but good things about David from his supervisor. In fact, he was one of her favorite employees.

Everything seemed to be going well until the night Keith and David took Gloria's car without permission. To make matters worse, Keith was driving without a license. I resented having to wake Gloria to go to the police station because of my brothers' irresponsibility. Fortunately for them, they got off with an insignificant punishment.

After that incident, David continued to refuse to follow the rules. I had to ask him to leave. He moved in with his girlfriend, a woman whom I was less than thrilled about. She was nearly forty years old and had five kids; David was only eighteen. Soon after he moved in with her, he was terminated from Children's Hospital.

The day after David left, Keith took Gloria's car without asking again, and this time, he hit a drunk pedestrian. I was terrified that we were going to lose everything we had, but, fortunately, no lawsuit was filed against us. Clearly, it was time for Keith to leave as well—this time for good. I gave Keith a bus ticket back to North Carolina. Shortly after he left, he was involved in an altercation, was stabbed multiple times, and was left for dead. Keith survived his injuries, but since that day, I've been on pins and needles, worrying that a call will come, giving me the worst news imaginable. It has become clear to me that I have nothing else to offer him.

I believe that was the knockout punch for our relationship; we barely speak to each other anymore.

We occasionally talk on the phone *maybe* every other year. He has no stable telephone number, so communication happens basically when he calls me. He seems, nevertheless, to be doing okay. I resent that our relationship became a casualty of the foster care system.

About the time that David and Keith transitioned out of our house, my grandmother started having problems with my sister Shanique. Grandma and I talked on the phone every day about everything, but one thing we spent a lot of time discussing was strategies to ensure that my sister successfully transitioned to adulthood and did not get jacked up by some dude before she graduated from high school. That goal was enough to create a strong bond between us. My grandmother was becoming fed up with Shanique and finally sent her to live with Gloria and me. Unfortunately, we were not as successful with her as we had hoped to be.

While Gloria and I were at work one day, we left Shanique to babysit Tiffany, Shane Rico, Brittney, and Courtney. When I got home from work, Shanique was nowhere to be found, and Tiffany was playing with the kitchen stove. When I confronted Shanique about her behavior, she simply shrugged her shoulders and said "So?" I went bonkers. I had flashbacks of our mother leaving Keith and me unattended. I simply lost it. That was the end of her stay. She was back in New York in less than a week's time.

Shortly after that, I received a late-night call from my grandmother. My Aunt Cookie (Sylvia) had been found dead outside a four-story building in Harlem. Her death was treated as a homicide at first, but then authorities concluded that she might have jumped. I don't know if we'll ever know for sure. I told Grandma that I would pay for Aunt Cookie's funeral, which was my way of doing for my mother's sister what I would have wanted to do for my mom. It was my opportunity for closure. At the funeral, I saw my aunt's son, Omar, for the first time in more than fourteen years. I had often asked Grandma about him, but she had refused to put us in touch.

Omar was a handful, and Grandma knew I would probably try to take on that responsibility as well. He was living in a group home and was bitter and filled with rage. I'd told Grandma repeatedly that maybe Omar needed me, because I could understand what he was going through, but Grandma insisted that I didn't need to take on anything else.

Whether Grandma liked it or not, I was determined to speak with Omar. He barely remembered me, but I remembered him well. He was the oldest of Aunt Cookie's five children, all of whom had been in foster care at one point or another. At first, I just promised to stay in touch with him. Then I invited him to come back to Maryland with me so that we could get to know each other better. The folks at the group home thought coming with me had to be better than what awaited Omar back in the rough neighborhood where he lived. Omar was a tough guy and had secured a place on several "Most Wanted" neighborhood lists.

After the funeral, I returned home with Omar. With a telephone number given to him by his stepfather, he hoped to reunite with his siblings. He was heartbroken to discover that he had a wrong number and no clue how to contact his brothers and sisters. Thank goodness he was at my house when he realized this and not in New York by himself. There is no telling how he would have dealt with his anger if I had not been there for him.

I didn't realize it when I invited him home, but I learned from his group home that Omar's last hope to turn his life around was a program called Glenn Mills in Pennsylvania. Gloria and I promised Omar that if he successfully completed Glenn Mills, he would always have a family standing beside him and that as long as he was enrolled, we would visit him regularly. A little more than two years later, with all promises kept, including regular home visits with us on weekends and holidays, Omar graduated from Glenn Mills with his high school diploma and a GED. Gloria and I were so proud of him, and we knew that we had been used to transform a life from pain to promise.

Because Omar had had hope, he had believed that voice deep inside that inspired him to try, so he hadn't given up on himself, and we hadn't give up on him either. The unleashed hope he received gave him the ability to discover his dreams. When Omar came back to live with us after graduation, I helped him get a job at Children's Hospital, and he performed in an exemplary manner. Eventually, he left our home and got a place of his own with his girlfriend.

Gloria and I felt like we were part of both success stories and continual challenges. Although Shane Rico continued to struggle, when he was twelve, our second son, David, arrived. We thought that having a brother—one who was also adopted—would take the pressure off of Shane Rico, but instead, his outbursts escalated.

Before the adoption, I had received a call from a friend who worked at the local child and family services agency; he told me they had a kid who would be perfect for our family. The child had been featured on a local television newscast, and my friend sent me a copy of the videotape. As soon as Gloria and I saw it, we fell in love with fourteen-year-old David.

Grandma was visiting at the time, so I asked her what she thought. She said, "If I could raise six, you can raise five." She had to be kidding. I hoped she did not think somehow that raising five children was any less daunting than raising six. But what I thought she really meant was that many others before me had endured raising large families with less resources. My grandmother often reminded me that I have the "stuff" strong men are made of. As I may question my capacity from time to time, it certainly helps to hear firsthand, from someone who has been through the worst of times, that hope endures all things.

I asked Tiffany about her feelings, and she responded just as a teenage girl would, "He's cute. I'll be very popular at school."

For me, the most moving part of the tape was David's response when the reporter asked why, at fourteen, David still wanted to be adopted. "When I'm thirty years old, I'm going to want a place to bring my children back to," David said.

I was thirty at the time, and I still felt like I had no place to bring my children back to. I felt an instant connection to him. The rest of the family saw the tape, we talked it over, and everybody agreed that David should become a part of our family. It was a unanimous decision. We didn't tell any of our friends or extended family right away, because we thought they would try to discourage us from adopting a black teenage boy, especially with three girls at home.

Born David Lewis, our son became David Lenard Aytch Salter, and Gloria and I were thrilled that we were able to give a home to another child who had been branded "hard to place."

When my father-in-law found out about our plans, he said, "What the hell are you trying to do to my daughter? Don't you all have enough kids?" I told him that he was selling himself short if he believed he had raised a child who wasn't an independent thinker. In fact, it was the gift of adoption that he had given her that compelled her to give that gift to others. He never uttered a word on the subject again.

A few months after David arrived, Grandma agreed to come down from New York to watch the children, so Gloria and I could take a trip together. The two of us hadn't had a break together in years. Finding someone to watch the kids for any length of time, since neither one of us had an extended family, was next to impossible. It's one reason we wanted a big family. We hoped our children would support each other when they became adults.

Thank God for Grandma. She seemed to always be there when we needed her. No excuses—she was just there. If Gloria was in the hospital for minor surgery, Grandma was there to nurse her back to health. If Gloria was out of town on business, Grandma would come down to give me a hand, because she knew I was hopeless without my wife.

As young as Grandma claimed to be, her true age was beginning to show by the time of this trip. I was reluctant to ask her to watch the children, but we really needed the respite. Off we went to Texas on a business trip for Gloria with me along for company. We weren't gone more than twenty-four hours when the telephone rang. It was Grandma calling from our house to inform us that there was a big problem. In the background, I could hear glass smashing onto the floor and objects crashing against the wall. Shane Rico was out of control. I instructed her to have David contain him and call the police. Never could I have imagined that I would call the police on my own child, but it was necessary to protect him and everyone else in the house.

When the police arrived, I told them over the phone that, because my wife and I were away, my son needed to be removed from the house. The police officer said they would take him to the Juvenile Detention Center. Then, at my request, they put my son on the phone. He was sobbing uncontrollably. With as reassuring of a tone as I could muster, I told him we would straighten everything out when I got home, but for now because he could not keep himself safe, he had to go with the policeman. Like a wounded lamb, he said okay. The next morning, I was on a plane headed home. David did all he could to clean up the evidence of Shane Rico's rage, but there was no hiding it. Everything had changed, and our family would never be the same.

Our medical insurance would not cover the long-term residential treatment that Shane Rico needed. After moving from Prince George's County, Maryland, where services were abundant but the schools were second-rate, to Chantilly, Virginia, in Fairfax County, where the schools were good but services were nonexistent, we were told by a social worker that Shane Rico would get the comprehensive help he needed only if he was charged and convicted of assaulting his siblings. Then the county would be obligated to help us by using the Family Resource Assistance Team. When I arrived at the courthouse, the detective assured me that having him adjudicated would enable him to receive comprehensive psychiatric services. I wondered, *What's that about? Let's lock him up to make him eligible for treatment? What's the real motivation here?*

I should have been even more suspicious when the court social worker asked me, "Why would you want to keep a kid like this anyway?"

"Why?" I asked. "Because he's my kid!"

When I read Shane Rico's record, the social worker had written in the notes that I hadn't resolved my foster care issues. She didn't expect me to read that, I'm sure. Unfortunately, I saw it after I agreed to let them charge my son as a criminal. To see him hauled away in handcuffs was heartbreaking for both his mother and me. As a parent, I was ashamed and remorseful; I felt that I had failed him.

What was even worse was that none of the services promised were ever delivered. After attending meeting after meeting, opening ourselves up to inquiry after inquiry as if Shane Rico were the only child we had at home, and after adhering to the requirements of the county and attending meetings and hearings, our son received not one county service. In fact, the county demanded that the District of Columbia pay for his care under the adoption subsidy agreement (which the city initially refused to honor) and threatened to remand Shane Rico to foster care and to come after us for his board if DC did not come through. The latter option would have bankrupted us and put the rest of the children at risk.

This cannot be happening, I thought. I went to the District of Columbia Child and Family Services, which was under receivership at the time and threatened to call a press conference unless they followed through with the services promised. The staff reexamined their obligation under the subsidy agreement and decided that it was in all of our best interests for them to honor it. The agency has since had a leadership change and is now being administered by a very capable and energetic visionary.

We ultimately found Kids Peace for Children in Crisis in Allentown, Pennsylvania. We visited and decided that the atmosphere and treatment program would help Shane Rico, so we transferred him there. It was hard making six-hour round trips between Virginia and Pennsylvania every other weekend, but we refused to miss any scheduled visits. After several years, we found a treatment facility much closer to home.

I wanted a sign from Shane Rico that he wanted to come back home, but he barely progressed through the different levels of his treatment program. Finally, I asked myself if we had let the situation go on for too long and if he was more comfortable in an institution than with us. Even though he repeatedly declared that he looked forward to coming home someday, as soon as he had progressed far enough to earn home privileges, he would have a setback. It looked like self-sabotage to me. No matter what, we were determined to remain his parents and to continue visiting him indefinitely, if that's what it took. Fortunately, when he moved closer, we could see him every Sunday and sometimes during the week. It was not unusual for Gloria to drop by for lunch when her schedule permitted.

Over time, we did notice significant improvement in his behavior. I'm sure the increased visits had plenty to do with that. He started earning passes for home visits, but unbelievably, his probation officer would not authorize him to leave the facility. I hit the roof. I informed the hospital that I was no longer authorizing the probation officer to review any information in my son's medical record if that review was going to be used for punitive reasons that were a direct contradiction to his therapeutic needs. Well, that was the beginning of a battle. I had no idea what I was in for. The probation officer subpoenaed me into court along with the CEO of the hospital. Cash-strapped from other associated expenses, I entered the courtroom with only faith as my legal counsel.

The county attorney represented Shane Rico. I thought it was amusing that my son had an attorney, but that I was there protecting his interests without one. The probation officer pleaded his case to the judge, regarding the importance of access to his medical records, and I responded with our view of the situation.

The judge began lecturing me from the bench, saying that probation was the only way that a sixteen-year-old child was going to comply with treatment.

After initially being polite and not getting my point across, I thought I had nothing to lose. I interrupted the judge and said, "Your Honor, you are obviously not hearing me."

There was dead silence in the courtroom. I got the courage to continue and said, "That's what he has parents for."

I then reminded the judge that we had brought this matter before the court, and that the only reason we had done so was to try to get him the care he needed.

"Well, your Honor," I went on to say, "he hasn't received any of the care they promised, and I'm asking you, in light of those facts, to close this case."

It was obvious that the judge was caught off guard.

"You mean the original incident happened in your home?"

"Yes, Your Honor," I said.

"You brought the matter before the court?"

"Yes, Your Honor."

With gavel in hand, he uttered, "Case dismissed."

I heard Gloria make a loud outburst, and then she started to cry. The CEO of the hospital cried as well. They kept saying I was awesome. I felt like some kind of hero for a minute, but I knew who the real hero was. It was someone much bigger than me. It was a miracle. I could not even remember what I had said or where the words came from. I was happy that a wrong had been made right and that all of those county workers were finally out of our lives. We could focus exclusively on our son's healing.

Shane Rico is now an adult, working with computers, living in New York, and doing unbelievably well. It meant the world to him to know that, although he wasn't able to live at home for a while, he mattered to someone.

Because he had consistently someone to advocate for him vigorously and to love him unconditionally, Shane Rico knew the benefit of a family while he was on his road to healing. Every child deserves at least that much. Considering everything he's had to overcome to get where he is, I am so proud of Shane Rico. So many people his age have had so much more given to them and have thrown it away. Shane Rico is using everything he has and is making the most of it.

There was a time while going through this that I spent feeling angry about my experiences with Shane Rico. I asked God, "Why me? Why, after all that I have already been through in my own childhood, would you have me endure this with an adopted son?" I asked God how he could expect me to continue to motivate people to adopt when we'd had such a traumatic experience.

Years later, after much agony and pain because of our struggles with Shane Rico, the answer came. There was purpose in my pain. It would have been very easy, given all that I had experienced as a child in foster care, to ask people to adopt or give a child what I had never had and always wanted. But having lived through an adoption experience that included love, disappointment, heartache, and then triumph, I could go out and say, "When it's at its worst, don't you dare give up. You may get tired; you might burn out and have to take a break, but don't you dare give up. You may have to parent some of our special-needs adopted children unconventionally, just as you would a special-needs birth child who can't be cared for at home, but don't ever stop being a parent." That was the powerful lesson my experience with Shane Rico Jr. taught me.

As grown men, people like Shane Rico and I are responsible for our lives and for the choices we make. I will not stop striving to be the best person I can be. I refuse to let pain from my past become my prison. Pain can kill your spirit, or it can be your power to unleash your purpose. It is all about the choices you make. What you choose determines how much of life you will enjoy, how much you will accomplish, and how purposeful your life will be.

Chapter 9
A CHANGE IS GONNA COME

It's been too hard living,
But I'm afraid to die,
Because I don't know what's up there beyond the sky.
It's been a long, a long time coming,
But I know a change gonna come. Oh yes, it will.
—Sam Cooke

While I worked at Children's Hospital, I saw vast numbers of babies abandoned by substance-abusing parents. There was a shortage of adoptive and foster care families available for those children. As a result, the children spent the early months of their lives in hospitals. I couldn't help but think, *Surely, there must be something I can do.*

I decided to call one of the local nonprofit agencies, For Love of Children (FLOC). I told FLOC's foster home recruiter, Valli Matthews, my story about growing up in foster care and about how much I didn't want that experience for those boarder babies. The pain and consequences of not having a permanent home are things no child should experience.

Ms. Matthews invited me to go on the *Cathy Hughes Morning Show* on WOL radio in Washington DC to help recruit families. Pleased with the outcome of the radio interview, Valli then asked me to sit on a training panel for foster parents. Shortly afterward, I began receiving invitations to speak at various conferences around the country, where social workers, administrators, foster families, adoptive families, and youth came together to advocate for children in need of homes.

My childhood psychologist, Dr. Lewis, heard that I was coming to

Albany, New York, to give a speech about my experiences in foster care, and she wrote to me. I still have the wonderful letter she sent.

I thanked her for believing in me when no one else had, and I promised that I would continue to make her proud. Dr. Lewis told me that my roommate from the Rego Park Group Home, Kenny, had asked about me, and she helped me get in touch with him. Kenny was completing graduate school in California at the time and wanted to come back East. I invited him to stay with my family and me, and he accepted.

We had a wonderful reunion, but I was shocked that, like my brother Keith, Kenny felt I had abandoned him, only that time it was when I left the group home for college. I'd never realized how much I meant to him, but when you're transitioning out of a group home to adulthood, your sole focus is on survival. I was seventeen and on my own. I had bigger issues than what was going on in the group home. The kids left behind had guaranteed shelter, at least. In retrospect, I understand, but all he had to do was write to me, and I would definitely have written back. I think he still lives in the Washington DC area, but we don't keep in touch—a fact that saddens me.

The speaking circuit has been wonderful. I've met some fascinating people, who are very committed to better outcomes for youth. I've met some awful ones, too—many are driven more by power than by the opportunity to promote healing and transformation in our communities and our children. It's always refreshing when I get the chance to be in the company of people who genuinely care about kids, people who are willing to break down whatever barriers exist to make things right.

On my way to one engagement in Seattle, I remembered hearing that Reverend Cameron, my former dad, had relocated to Seattle and had died of a heart attack. I decided to look up his mother and sister to see how they were doing and to let them know how I was doing. I had no idea how to get in touch with them, but I remembered that he had always talked about how much he had loved being a member of Mt. Zion Baptist Church when he was a little boy. I called Mt. Zion, explained that I had been one of Reverend Cameron's foster children, that I had recently learned of his death, and that I wanted to know how to reach his family.

The woman on the other end of the phone said, "Reverend Cameron isn't dead."

He was alive, well, and working as a school principal. Talk about a surprise! I was so thrilled that Reverend Cameron was okay, but I was also nervous about seeing him after all we'd gone through. With my friend Jackie providing moral support, I decided to pay a visit to Reverend Cameron's school.

When he emerged from his office, he was surprised to see me. He embraced me warmly and seemed genuinely pleased. We spoke briefly, and I invited him to come hear me speak. He couldn't commit, but he said he would try to make it. I said good-bye to Reverend Cameron, not knowing if I'd ever see him again. But it felt good to let him see that I'd made it and that I was doing fine.

Just as I began my speech at the One Church, One Child Conference, Reverend Cameron strolled into the hotel ballroom. I was startled at first but remained focused on my remarks. As I acknowledged him from the podium, it dawned on me that many of the rules he had imposed on me, which I had rebelled against, were the same rules that I was imposing on Tiffany. During my remarks I acknowledged that I wasn't able to receive the love he was trying to give me when I was in his home. Knowing how much I still desired a relationship with a father, I asked him, "Is it too late for me to ask you to be my dad?"

"No, it's not," he said, and in that moment we connected.

This personal reunion and speech had a far greater than expected effect on some members of the audience. One minister declared that he was going to go searching for his long-lost son. Father Clement committed to strengthening his relationship with his son Joey. Many fathers decided to have better relationships with their children. How powerful! What a wonderful sense of purpose that experience gave me.

Chapter 10
YOU WERE LOVED

We all wanna make a place in this world.
We all want our voices to be heard.
Everyone wants a chance to be someone.
We all have dreams we need to dream.
—Diane Warren and Whitney Houston

An unexpected gift that came from my growing closeness with my grandmother was the stories she was able to tell me about my family. Our relationship has allowed her to be honest about her feelings and the choices she made before and after my birth. The stories she has told me about that time have helped me not only to understand and respect her but also to realize who I am. Her revelations have also equipped me to make it impossible to let others define me ever again. As I recount some of what she shared with me, perhaps you too will understand how multigenerational pain contributed to the abandonment of my brother and me and understand what fueled my determination to break that cycle with my children, my siblings, and my cousins.

Perhaps there's someone in your life whom you can try to understand better so your own cycle of healing can begin.

♦ ♦ ♦

Sherry's grandmother Flossy was a New York City showgirl. It was her goal-driven, succeed-at-any-cost attitude that made her walk away from her husband and infant daughter to further her showgirl career of providing entertainment for the merchant marines. On a blustery winter day, Flossy wrapped little Sandra warmly in a blanket and left the child on her Aunt Gertie's doorstep. Flossy walked away and never looked back. Gertie was shocked that Flossy would do such a thing, but thankfully, she was happy to have Sandra to rear as her own.

Sandra, my grandmother, grew up, following her mother's colorful career, but Flossy showed no interest in her. In fact, she appeared to go out of her way to act is if Sandra had never been born. It shattered Sandra's heart to think that the woman who had given birth to her could deny her. Aunt Gertie did her best to counteract the damage Flossy's rejection had done. As often as possible, she reassured Sandra that she was beautiful and told her repeatedly that she could be anything she wanted to be. Aunt Gertie told Sandra that she could even be a showgirl, just like her mother, if she wanted.

"I'll be anything but like my mother," Sandra insisted.

The years of abandonment and neglect changed Sandra's feelings for her mother from disappointment to hatred. However, she adored her Aunt Gertie, and Sandra was devastated when Gertie suddenly died. Sandra was just eighteen, and the only mother she had ever known was gone. She was alone, scared, and broke. She had no marketable skills other than the domestic abilities she had acquired at home.

In her vulnerable state, the first man who came along—Leroy, a high, yellow brother with freckles—had no trouble charming the stockings off her. Their marriage didn't last, however, because Leroy was abusive to Sandra from the start. When Sandra returned home from the hospital after having their first child, Leroy raped her, rupturing her so terribly that she had to be rushed back to the hospital. The doctors and nurses couldn't believe the damage Leroy's attack had done.

Sandra eventually left Leroy and moved to New Jersey, but it wasn't long before she took Leroy back and allowed him and his mother to move in with her. That turned out to be the worst mistake of her life. Leroy drank excessively and beat her up regularly. She didn't know which was more painful: getting her ass beaten or the humiliation of Leroy's mother looking on with approval.

"A man's got to do what a man's got to do," his mother would say. Sandra always knew that Leroy's mother felt that she wasn't good enough for him, and finally, Sandra had come to the conclusion that her mother-in-law was right. She knew she didn't deserve to be abused, but Sandra didn't think she could do much better than Leroy, so she tried to make the marriage work. Mostly, she stayed because she didn't want to abandon her child the way her mother, Flossy, had abandoned her.

Confused and conflicted, Sandra had another child with Leroy. She left him again, but he found out where she was living, kicked in the door, and carried her and the two children back to New Jersey, where they sold bootleg liquor for a living. Their third child (my mother, Sherry) was born shortly thereafter.

Sandra, Leroy, and their three children eventually moved to Hartford, Connecticut. During an argument, Leroy threw his wife out of a moving car, and she rolled down into a ditch. A passerby saved her life by calling an ambulance. The only good thing about that incident was that Leroy never found her again. Sandra didn't know if Leroy never tried to locate her because he thought she was dead or because he was afraid she would call the police. Whatever the reason, she was at last free of Leroy. It didn't take her long to find enough courage to sever the remaining ties as she returned to New Jersey for her children one weekend while Leroy was out of town.

Sandra met a new love, and although it didn't last, she had her fourth child with him. She became an exotic dancer to feed her children. While dancing in nightclubs, she met a sailor named Eric and had her fifth and sixth children with him. Eventually, Sandra got her own place in the South Bronx.

Although she was a single mother of six by then, Sandra still thought she was a little, hot thing. Her new boyfriend, Vernon, must have thought likewise, because he would think nothing of jumping on the subway on the Upper West Side where he lived and traveling to the South Bronx for an occasional booty call.

But by then, Sandra had hardened over the years and didn't take crap from anyone. She was especially protective of her kids. Unlike the abusive relationship of her first marriage, the subsequent men never treated her badly. When it came to her kids, it was not unusual to find Sandra in the street, fighting with someone who had messed with one of her babies. Whether they were right or wrong, she believed, as a result of her life experiences, that family members stick up for one another no matter what. All the kids understood and were reminded of this family value every day before they walked out the door.

While she sought to love and protect all of the children, it was no secret that Sandra's boys were her favorites. Her sons could do no wrong. However, when it came to her daughter, Sherry, she was particularly protective. I guess you have to be when your daughter is one of the prettiest girls in the neighborhood and, at thirteen, one of the last remaining virgins. Every little roughneck on the block had staked his claim to Sherry. At thirteen years old, Sherry was arrested for stealing, but Sandra was certain that Sherry had been set up, never doubting her innocence for one minute.

The detective was hauling Sherry off in handcuffs, when he accidentally hit her in the eye. Instinctively and with no regard for the fact that the officer was carrying a gun, Sandra picked up the closest frying pan and hit him on the head. All hell broke loose. In the end, both mother and daughter were handcuffed and taken to the police station. The judge released Sandra, but sent Sherry away for a year to Hudson Juvenile Home for Girls.

After Sherry was released from Hudson, Sandra really tightened the reins on her, refusing to let Sherry out of her sight. Boyfriends were out of the question for Sherry until Sandra's boyfriend Vernon suggested that he introduce Sherry to his little brother David. With Sherry always in the house, Vernon couldn't get enough "private time" with her mother. David could keep Sherry busy while Vernon got busy with Sandra. At first, Sandra wasn't too keen on the idea.

"I ain't having any stuff in my house," Sandra warned him.

"You don't have a thing to worry about," Vernon assured her. "Dee Dee ain't anything to worry about, and you know I'll jack him up if he tries anything. Besides, it's time for Sherry to have a little freedom. You can't keep that girl locked up like that."

Eventually, Vernon got his way, and Sandra allowed Dee Dee to come around with Vernon and keep company with Sherry. Dee Dee turned on the charm and hit it off with Sandra immediately. His gift of gab gave her the impression that he was a good kid. The truth of the matter was that sixteen-year-old Dee Dee was nothing but a smooth-talking, dope-dealing hustler and a master thief. In his short life, he had already spent as much time in juvenile detention as he had spent at home. But Sherry found his charm irresistible, and none of the other boys in the neighborhood stood a chance after that.

When Dee Dee discovered that Sherry was not only beautiful but could sing too, he melted like butter. It wasn't long after she met Dee Dee that Sherry fell in love, surrendered her virginity, and became pregnant with me. It all happened with Vernon and Sandra locked in the next room, too busy with each other to realize that I was being conceived on the living room couch.

Sherry was terrified of what her mother's response would be when she found out she was pregnant. She knew that Sandra had big dreams for her. The thought of Sherry repeating her mother's mistakes was unacceptable to her mother. Sherry couldn't stop thinking about all the times her mother had warned her not to get pregnant and what Sandra had threatened to do if any daughter of hers dared to disobey.

"You better not bring any babies up in here," Sandra had said. "If any of you come in here pregnant, I'm telling you, I'll beat it out of you."

If there was one thing Sherry knew about her mother, it was that she said what she meant and meant what she said. She had to keep her pregnancy a secret from her mother for her own safety and for the safety of her baby. A neighbor finally gave away Sherry's secret. She commented to Sandra that Sherry seemed to be getting a bit big and asked, "Girl, you sure she ain't pregnant?"

"Hell no! I don't let Sherry out of my sight," Sandra insisted. "Besides, she knows I'd beat her ass down if she tried to come in here with a baby."

But later that evening, as soon as Sherry walked in the door, Sandra made Sherry take off her clothes, and there was no doubt that Sherry was very pregnant. The sight of Sherry's bulging tummy sent Sandra into a hysterical rage. She started pounding on Sherry with her fists and screaming at the top of her lungs, "I'm gonna beat you till it drops out of you."

Sherry fell to the floor and curled herself into a knot, trying desperately to protect her child from her mother's punches, kicks, and stomps, crying and begging her to quit. It seemed the beating was never going to end, until finally, exhausted and out of breath, Sandra stopped. The terrible abuse was surely enough to cause Sherry to miscarry, but amazingly, both my mother and I made it through. I had won my very first fight for survival.

Having failed in her attempt to beat the baby out of her daughter, Sandra plotted to have Sherry's pregnancy terminated.

"You are not bringing no baby in here. We are getting rid of it," she told her daughter.

Sandra made an appointment and dragged Sherry to an illegal, backdoor, abortion house. They had only just begun prepping her for the procedure when Sherry jumped off the table, grabbed her clothes, and bolted out of the door.

"You are not going to kill my baby," she screamed as she left the abortion house, putting on her clothes as she ran. Eventually, Sandra had to accept the fact that Sherry was determined to keep her baby and that I was going to be born.

Things didn't look good at all when the time came for Sherry to deliver. She was just fifteen years old, with blood pressure so high that the doctors didn't think she would survive the birth, although they thought they could save the baby. A priest was called to perform last rites.

Sandra nearly collapsed when she heard this. She couldn't believe her daughter was near death, giving birth to a child Sandra didn't approve of or welcome. Sandra went to the chapel and prayed for Sherry's life. "God, if you have to take one of them, please take this baby and let Sherry live," she pleaded. And God did what she asked, and more.

Sherry miraculously survived the life-threatening complications, and on November 21, 1963, at eleven twenty pm, I was born as David Earl Williams Jr., weighing in at seven pounds eleven ounces. My name was changed from David to Shane, thanks to Grandma. Sandra hated my father so much that she told the hospital records clerk that she would "kick her ass" if David Williams showed up on that birth certificate. Wisely, the terrified clerk chose not to risk a confrontation and issued my birth certificate with the name Shane Lenard Salter, per my grandmother's instructions. The choice of Shane was inspired by the old western movie starring Allan Ladd, and Lenard was to honor my uncle, John Lenard. Shane, a variation of John, means "God's most gracious gift" in Greek; in Hebrew, it means "beautiful." Salter is my grandmother's last name. The first Mr. Salter had been a white Englishman from a family of salt miners who had married a freed slave when he settled in the United States.

A few years after I was born, my mother applied for public assistance, and we moved to our own apartment in the basement of a brownstone in Harlem. It was my father, Dee Dee, who introduced my mother to drugs, which eventually led to her heroin addiction. With Dee Dee in and out of jail, my mother met Norman, a much older man, who tried unsuccessfully to help her get off drugs. Norman fathered my mother's second son, Keith, who was born in 1966.

Of course, I knew none of this story while growing up. All I had known was that my family wasn't there. I didn't understand for many years what had happened to my mother or why she hadn't come back for us. Now I know, and I understand. While I don't excuse or justify my mother's actions, I certainly understand her pain, and I understand how it all happened in spite of her best intentions.

I have learned from the pain in my grandmother's eyes that, because she was abandoned as an infant, she couldn't give my mother what she needed. She wanted to break the cycle. She did the best with what she had, and it just wasn't enough.

That's why it's so crucial that all children get from us what they will need to give to their children someday. Love them, and they will know how to give love. Encourage them, and they will know how to give encouragement. See the best in them, and they will see the best in others. Tell them they are beautiful and strong and have a purpose, and they will treat others as if they are beautiful and strong and have purposes. Give them a safe place to call home, and they will make sure they create a safe place to call home. Show them that, no matter how dark the moment, how powerful the enemy, you can overcome any trouble, and they will be rooted in the knowledge that tomorrow is a new beginning and is worth living for.

Child abuse and neglect are largely an intergenerational problem. Although it is clear that the nature and severity of some types of abuse can be caused by mental illness or character disorders, many parents who abuse and neglect their children were abused themselves. They try to cope with environmental stresses and the demands of parenting, but they have few resources to meet those challenges with and many terrible memories to cope with. When I understood this truth, the knowledge helped me to both open the door to true forgiveness and recognize and confront my own demons.

Chapter 11
LIKE A MOTHERLESS CHILD: A LONG WAY FROM HOME

Lord, I'm lost; I can't find my way.
I'm dealing with the struggles in my day-to-day
My soul is weak, and I want to be strong;
I try to runaway, but I've been running too long
-Anonymous

On Christmas night in 1999, I received a call from Mom Jenkins who told me that her son Robbie had died. I offered to go home to be with her and the family. I was mystified when she told me not to.

"It's the holiday. We can't do anything right now," she said. "I'll call you with the arrangements."

A few days later, she left me a voice message, referring to herself as Doris, which was very strange. She was always Mom to Grandma, my children, and me—never Doris. I attributed her behavior to stress.

She asked me to write Robbie's obituary, and I immediately agreed, excited that she wanted me to perform such an important task, thrilled to know that I was valued and still fit in. I went to work on it right away. I was so proud of what I wrote and was eager to show it to her. I was surprised when she became irritated that my first draft stated that Robbie had died "after a long illness."

"Take that out," she snapped.

I was puzzled; it had been a long illness. But I put my feelings aside. After all, he was *her* son, and maybe I wasn't supposed to be grieving, because he was not my natural brother.

When I placed a hand on her back to comfort her during the funeral, she whispered, "Don't touch me." At that point, I knew she was angry with me, but I didn't know why.

On the way back from the cemetery after Robbie's burial, I asked Mom Jenkins if I could have a small token from Robbie's apartment as a keepsake. She snapped at me again, saying, "He didn't have anything. I don't know what you want."

At that point, I decided it was best not to say anything more to her. I thought I understood the depth of her pain, because I too was in pain. But it seemed much more than that. Could it be that the mother who had raised me was angry because it was Robbie who was dead instead of me? If not, it sure felt like it. I was not supposed to be the one who survived. I was not supposed to be the one who completed college. But they had helped to make all that possible. I knew that I wouldn't have survived without them. Mom and Dad Jenkins meant the world to me, and I thought I meant just as much to them. I never missed an opportunity to show the depth of my gratitude.

But it seemed that I was stuck in time. Everything and everyone had moved on in the Jenkins family after Keith and I left, except me. Keith had wanted to stay, and when we didn't, I never understood why he wouldn't keep in touch with the Jenkinses, with any of the families, or with Grandma. Whenever we left a home and said good-bye, Keith meant good-bye and didn't look back. If you sent him packing, he accepted that finality.

I just didn't see things that way as a child. To me, Mom and Dad Jenkins were still my parents. But to them, the day Keith and I were sent off to the failed adoption, I became nothing more than their former foster child. How could that be after all those years of treating me like a son—Catholic schools, reconstructive dental work, and so forth? The Jenkins family had been the most stable force throughout my life. I had always stayed in contact with them, giving periodic updates on my progress and accomplishments. Had I been creating a fantasy to help myself feel safe? Had that been one of my efforts to latch onto somebody else's family to help with my transition to adulthood? Had the accomplishments I had shared with them over the years, as any normal child would, added insult to injury, because Robbie had been struggling? Was I supposed to be out of their lives? I had simply thought they would be proud of the return on their investment, and

I had wanted to hear someone who had known me as a little boy say, "I'm proud of you, son."

One of the reasons I had gone into healthcare was that I wanted Ma Jenkins to feel she had influenced me, because she was a registered nurse. If there was any place I thought I had identity, any place where I could be myself and get love and acceptance, it was with the Jenkinses. What happened at the funeral was so painful that I couldn't face it. I certainly wasn't able to understand it. I couldn't even talk about it for a long time. I dealt with it in therapy, but it's probably still inside me somewhere.

Ma Jenkins and I didn't speak at all until five years later, when I happened to run into her at a wedding of a friend in Washington DC. It was ironic that she and I knew the same people. I could never have imagined that she would be there. I became very nervous, wondering how she would react to me that time. After some folks in the family encouraged us, we posed together for a couple of pictures. I gave her a hug, looked her dead in the eye, and told her what I felt in my soul, finishing with "No matter what, I still love you, and there's nothing you can do about it."

I don't know if she was embarrassed, overwhelmed, or what, but her only response was "You're squishing my glasses."

I later learned that, after Robbie's death, Dad Jenkins had taken seriously ill, which, sadly, meant that Mom Jenkins had spent all of her retirement caring for people she loved who were gravely ill—first her son, and then her husband.

I finally worked up the nerve to call her, and we actually had a good conversation about everything—except for the reason we didn't talk for all those years. We never got quite back to our old relationship, but I thought the healing process had begun until several years later on the Friday afternoon before Labor Day weekend.

On that day, I received a phone call at my office in Washington DC. It felt like déjà vu.

"Shane, this is Doris."

"Hi Mom," I said.

Without pause, she said, "Bob died last Sunday."

Because I could not allow her to diminish who he was to me, I asked, "You mean Dad?"

"Yeah," she said. "I couldn't find your telephone number, Shane," she continued. "Sorry I couldn't reach you earlier, but the wake is this Saturday, and the Mass will be on Labor Day."

My thoughts started racing. It took her five days to call me? Why? It seemed twisted, but she appeared to have no regard for the effect that the death of the one man who had always believed in and understood me would have on me. Had she just blocked out all those years, or had she forgotten that I was the same person as the child they had both helped raise? Although I was all grown-up then, I was more grateful and loyal than the universe had words to capture—and still am today. I continue to see Mom and Dad Jenkins through the eyes of a child who sought safe harbor and was given it by them. She is my mother, and he will always be my daddy.

"I will be there, Mom," I told her.

I hung up the phone and let the tears flow, before calling a good friend and sobbing uncontrollably. Afterward, I regained my composure and left for what would be the most painful Labor Day weekend of my life.

I thought I was prepared for anything, but not the heartache of being told that I had to ride in a van behind the family limousine, because there was no room left in the car. Beaten, bruised, maybe covered with scars too deep to camouflage, I still remained determined to comport myself with grace and dignity, determined to respect her grief and anger. There is one thing that is great about being an adult— you don't have to keep begging for unconditional love and acceptance. You don't have to keep calling and visiting all the time, as I had had to do when I was a kid in order to keep a roof over my head. I am learning to love and to accept myself unconditionally, which is good enough for now.

I just don't have the motivation to be the driver in relationships anymore. I noticed over the years that, if I didn't initiate contact, most of my relationships eventually dwindled away. Well lately, I've just let this one—and a lot of others—die.

There is one relationship, however, that no matter how much I wanted to, I just couldn't abandon. For a while after I ran away from my father, I was too afraid to visit him. While I was attending Elmira College, I heard that he had been stabbed nine times and had almost lost his life. But even then, I didn't try to get in touch; I was just too uncomfortable around him.

Finally, one summer when I returned from school, I decided to visit him. That was the day he drove me by an abandoned building in the Bronx. It was no ordinary place.

"The bodies of the men who tried to kill me are in that building," he boasted, pointing at a dilapidated garden apartment.

I knew about some of his other crimes, but a murderer? It was beyond belief. *I am the son of a murderer*, I kept telling myself.

Over the years, as I watched his progressive deterioration in health and self-esteem, I became sad, but I struggled with resentment and had no respect left for him. After my first daughter, Tiffany, was born, I refused to call him Dad and started calling him by his street name, Dee Dee. Now that I was a father with my own vision of what a father should be, I couldn't bring myself to call him Dad anymore.

Still, as I matured and grew spiritually, I found myself compelled to follow the command "Honor thy father and thy mother." I recognized that we are commanded to honor our parents, even if they fail to measure up to our expectations. I also realized that, at the end of my own earthly journey, I wouldn't be judged by what kind of father I had but by what kind of son I'd been. After that revelation, our relationship improved significantly. But the truth is that, when my father died, even though by then I could love him, I felt relieved. At the time of his death, his youngest child was two years old. I could only pray that no more of my family members would enter the foster care system or become addicted to drugs.

I always knew that I would be responsible for his funeral arrangements, and although finances were very tight in my house at the time, I did my duty. None of his siblings or family members would contribute to the expenses for one reason or another. To cut costs, I asked a friend who was an ordained minister to ride with me from Washington DC and to preside at my father's service. When she asked me what she should know about him, I told her the truth. My father had been a thief, a drug dealer, a drug addict, and a self-described murderer—not exactly a model father. I insisted that her eulogy be honest.

His sister agreed to dress him in a short-sleeve golf shirt, pants, and tennis shoes—the same outfit that he wore every day. He never looked more peaceful or better; he had no gray hairs and skin as smooth as silk.

At the service, the minister, Reverend Lassiter, did an awesome job. She kept it real, just as I had asked her. It was the right choice. Everyone appreciated and recognized the person we were talking about and the soul we were praying for. If there is such a thing as a good funeral, that was one.

There was no disguising the facts of my background. And that's why my great-grandmother begged me to live my life, to leave my family alone, and to never look back. She thought that this estranged family of mine was only going to bring me down. However, I am who I am, and it's not in my nature to turn my back on folks I care about. So I didn't follow her advice, and I continued to pursue relationships with as many members of my family as I could find.

When my great-grandmother died, sadly, she had lost most of her material wealth. As she had become less mobile, she had entrusted her possessions to a "friend," who robbed her blind. Even the baby grand piano was gone.

It was equally painful to watch my great-granddad slip away. Toward the end of his life, he developed Alzheimer's. As a result, he wasn't able to recognize me when I visited him in the hospital. He was the only one who had made me believe that I had been remembered while in foster care, and then he didn't know me anymore. That was hard. But I had memories to fall back on. Every time I looked at that old baby shoe, I remembered how he had thought about me and believed in me when that mattered the most. I made peace with his condition, realizing that it could not affect our relationship, and I accepted that my great-granddad was leaving us one day at a time. It was not long before he peacefully closed those bright eyes for the last time and left on his final journey.

Chapter 12
BORN FOR THIS

There's a time to live and a time to die.
So let's celebrate each moment of our life,
And if we ever lose our way because the heart is torn,
Never let it question why the reason we were born.
—Bee Bee Winans

Great-Granddad's vision of my life as transforming and redeeming is the greatness I believe that we can all achieve and that we are called to achieve. After leaving Children's Hospital (my first job after the navy), I began a professional career in child welfare and served as the chief operating officer of For Love of Children (FLOC). FLOC was one of the largest family support nonprofits in Washington DC. The position was an opportunity for me to develop patience, to confront the realities of how the system really worked, and to see the worst and best in people—all in the name of serving children.

Life came full circle. I was no longer the kid who was upset because, as soon as he started college, his group home bed was assigned to someone else. Now, as a child welfare administrator, I was the person who gave that bed away. To run my organization effectively, my job was to ensure that we maintained "maximum census for full reimbursement." In other words, many of my decisions were driven to meet payroll by keeping children in our foster care programs rather than the motivation to find permanent homes for them. I was also conflicted and disheartened by my agency's inability to offer additional support to the number of children seeking support after being discharged from our program without permanent homes. Is it any wonder that 45 percent of those leaving foster care become homeless within a year?

The CEO and I were as different as day and night, but we complemented each other. He was an incredible visionary from Kentucky, and I was an urban cowboy from the South Bronx. Fred was a passionate, no-frills advocate for children, and I learned a great deal while working with him.

After my tenure with FLOC, I served as the national director of the Marriott Foundation for People with Disabilities. That job was my introduction to corporate America. It was a challenge transitioning from a nonprofit, where the prevailing sentiment was "Can't we all just get along?" to Marriott, where I was regularly reminded that it didn't matter that we were a nonprofit organization, our service had to be run like an efficient business, just like every other subsidiary of the Marriott Corporation.

Shortly after arriving, the CEO took me to meet Richard Marriott and introduced me as the new national director. I shook Mr. Marriott's hand and gave him a hug. I hugged everybody and never thought anything of it. Apparently, that was not the Marriott culture. Pulling me aside, my CEO told me, "You should get to know people before you hug them."

I was mortified. My second day on the job, and I had already managed to ruin my career. For weeks, I replayed that scenario in my head, thinking what a fool I had made of myself, until I was told that the CEO had apologized for me the next time he saw Mr. Marriott, explaining that I had just come from the nonprofit community.

"That Shane is quite a hugger, isn't he?" he had said to Mr. Marriott.

I'm sure he was surprised to hear Mr. Marriott say, "Yes, and we sure could use a lot more hugging around here."

My experience at Marriott turned out to be wonderful, and by the time I left, we were a hugging foundation.

I then became the director of the Freddie Mac Foundation. The greatest outcome of that experience was the expansion of my family. One Sunday morning, I was watching the repeat of WRC's "Wednesday's Child," featuring two brothers in need of a family. Moyé and Nigel were three and five years old at the time and reminded me of Keith and me. I instantly fell in love with them. Not only were they adorable but here was an opportunity to keep two little brothers together. Hard though I tried, I couldn't put them out of my mind.

I spoke to "Saint" Gloria, making the case that our influence could help the two boys grow into healthy, productive young men. Besides, Tiffany was going to graduate from high school in June, my son David had already graduated and moved into his own apartment, and Shane Rico was away. The only children left in our house were Brittney and Courtney. Although our home had seemed just the right size when we had purchased it, it felt very large. Surely, there was room for two more. Whenever I think back to those times, I can't help but laugh at myself. Who did I think I was? Mr. Josephine Baker?

We had moved from our home in Chantilly, Virginia, to a house in Ashburn, Virginia, because it had a mother-in-law suite for my grandmother, so she could move in with us when she became too old to live alone. That move meant that Tiffany had to attend a different high school for her senior year. I totally minimized her predicament because, except when I was with the Jenkins family, I had changed schools many times during my childhood. Initially, Tiffany said she didn't mind. Perhaps if I had stayed at one school as a teenager I'd have instinctively known that she really didn't mean that and that she was putting her own needs aside in favor of mine. Eventually, she admitted that she was angry with me. It was touch and go for a while—she struggled her entire senior year—but she made it.

Her graduation that June meant more to me than she could imagine. Not only was she officially launched, but she was the second generation of our family with a high school diploma. I also felt a tremendous sense of achievement, because I had kept the promise I had made to her at birth. I had never walked out on her and had been there from her infancy to her graduation. It wasn't always easy, but with our guardian angel Gloria by our side, we had made it.

My daughter never knew the kind of rejection and loneliness I had known, and she hadn't joined that 22 percent of teenage girls who become pregnant. Thus, we'd broken yet another generational curse. Tiffany decided to follow in my footsteps and enlisted in the navy after graduation. Two months later, Gloria also completed her life goal and earned her Master of Science degree in information technology from The American University. She had worked full-time at AT&T, attended graduate school full-time, and remained focused with a house full of children. How amazing and brilliant that woman is! I keep praying that the children will model her character, discipline, and brains.

Soon after Gloria's graduation, our two new sons arrived. I was so gung ho about being a new dad that I took a couple weeks of paternity leave. For me, two weeks off from work was unprecedented. It was like an extra Christmas, and the twinkle in Moyé and Nigel's eyes said it all. Looking at my beautiful family reminded me of how much I had overcome in my life and of how fortunate I was to have found a way out of the despair I had known.

Later in my tenure at the Freddie Mac Foundation, I was extremely pleased to be able to channel funds from the foundation to New York's Administration for Children Services (ACS), the same foster care system that had taken care of me. Formerly known as the Bureau of Child Welfare, ACS was under the leadership of Nicolas Scopetta and William Bell at the time, and I developed a good relationship with both of them. Nick was also a product of the foster care system, and I was happy that someone who had experienced foster care firsthand was leading the system in New York.

Through my friendships at ACS, I also developed a relationship with Mayor Rudi Giuliani. New York City had made a number of important reforms in foster care during his tenure, and I was able to convince the Freddie Mac Foundation to honor the mayor for his work on behalf of New York's foster children. Can you imagine what I felt when a *New York Post* editorial, "Credit Where Credit's Due" on December 13, 2000, reported, "An independent blue-ribbon panel is calling the Giuliani administration's effort to combat child abuse and neglect remarkable. After two years of study, the panel recently released a comprehensive, good news report.... The results are clear: Real changes are possible at city agencies. Congratulations to all concerned. Your hard work has paid off."

On February 3, 2005, I read in *The New York Times* an article by Leslie Kaufman, "2,200 children, or more than 10 percent of all those in foster care, will be transferred to agencies with the best track records in the city's annual performance review. The poorly rated agencies had serious shortcomings in such areas as recordkeeping, child safety, and monitoring the care of children placed with foster parents." When I went through the system, we were merely stuck. Agencies were not held to the same standards when I was growing up. It is encouraging to see that, after all these years, there is now greater oversight and accountability for the care provided to children. However, what saddens me is that the progress made still falls far short of the standard any of us should hold for raising children to successful adulthood.

I encouraged the CEO of Freddie Mac and the CEO of the foundation to host a grand reception in the mayor's honor at Battery Park and to present the mayor with an award. I had the pleasure of presenting that award and of introducing Mayor Giuliani, and I did so with tremendous enthusiasm. The ceremony was personal. My life's work culminated right there in that room in the park. I was able to go back home to New York City and to acknowledge the mayor of my city for leading one of the largest system reform efforts ever in child welfare.

During his acceptance speech, the mayor said to the crowd, "I think Shane Salter should run for mayor," and the crowd responded with thunderous applause. I relished that moment, but at the same time, I was aware that my boss at the foundation didn't like her subordinates getting an ounce more attention than she got, especially when *her* boss, the CEO of Freddie Mac, was present. I assured the audience that I was flattered but had no plans to leave Freddie Mac any time soon.

The mayor invited me back to New York a few weeks later for lunch with him, and we sat and talked in his office for more than two and a half hours. We exchanged philosophies on leadership and management, talking deeply about our challenges and successes. While I was there, I wanted someone to pinch me.

How did I go from being a foster child, whom everyone rejected, in New York to sitting and enjoying casual conversation and lunch with the mayor of New York? *If my friends could see me now!* I thought.

Nick Scopetta whispered afterward, "Those of us in the cabinet don't even get that much uninterrupted time with him. He really enjoyed talking with you." The whole experience is still amazing to me now, especially because September 11, 2001, was just a few months away, and Mayor Giuliani's life was about to be transformed once again.

Soon thereafter, the White House asked me to join President George W. Bush for the signing of the Safe and Stable Family Act. Returning to my office following the signing ceremony, I was informed by my boss that I had been terminated, effective that day and without severance pay. I could not believe it.

How painfully ironic, I thought, *to be witnessing the signing of the Safe and Stable Families Act that morning, only to have my family totally destabilized that afternoon.*

Honoraria from speaking engagements were not lucrative and consistent enough to support my family, which had been enlarged by two new sons—whom I desperately wanted to keep but whom I was no longer sure I could afford. All of this was circling in my head as I tried to figure out how to keep the news from my family—at least for one day—so we could celebrate Grandma's birthday. I knew it was going to be hard, but I didn't realize how hard until my doorbell rang in midafternoon, and I opened the door to find my office belongings being delivered in cardboard boxes.

My mind flashed back to all those times I had been thrown out of homes as a child. Dropping to my knees, I returned to the rock that is greater than I am.

I prayed, and through my prayers, God reminded me that everything I have, he gave to me. He had placed me in those circumstances to learn and to grow. My healing began when I acknowledged my pain and recognized that I couldn't control my life. That was someone else's job.

On my knees, I was reminded to remain steadfast, for no one could take from me that which is not theirs to give in the first place. I regained my determination to pick myself up and keep trying. I knew I just had to be patient and endure the pruning process. I was strengthened, as I hope you will be, through the power of the poem "If," by Rudyard Kipling, which is one of the signature poems of Alpha Phi Alpha.

If
Rudyard Kipling

Are losing theirs and blaming it on you;
If you can trust yourself when all men doubt you,
But make allowance for their doubting too:
If you can wait and not be tired by waiting,
Or being lied about, don't deal in lies,
Or being hated, don't give way to hating,

And yet don't look too good, nor talk too wise;

If you can dream—and not make dreams your master;
If you can think—and not make thoughts your aim,
If you can meet with Triumph and Disaster
And treat those two imposters just the same:
If you can bear to hear the truth you've spoken
Twisted by knaves to make a trap for fools,
Or watch the things you gave your life to, broken,
And stoop and build 'em up with worn-out tools;

If you can make one heap of all your winnings
And risk it on one turn of pitch-and-toss,
And lose, and start again at your beginnings
And never breathe a word about your loss:
If you can force your heart and nerve and sinew
To serve your turn long after they are gone,
And so hold on when there is nothing in you
Except the Will which says to them: "Hold on!"

If you can talk with crowds and keep your virtue,
Or walk with Kings—nor lose the common touch,
If neither foes nor loving friends can hurt you,
If all men count with you, but none too much:
If you can fill the unforgiving minute
With sixty seconds' worth of distance run,
Yours is the Earth and everything that's in it,
And—which is more—you'll be a Man, my son!

(Retrieved from http://en.wikisource.org/wiki/
IfpercentE2percent80percent94.)

I went to human resources to tell them that I had recently been diagnosed with ADD and placed on medication. My boss was aware of this, because she had, in fact, recommended that the doctor who had treated a family member with ADD. Within days of adjusting to my new medication, I was filled with hope the more ordered my thoughts became. On my new medication and in front of my peers while sitting in her office—my boss cursed me out, upon realizing that she had falsely accused me of something once again; that time was different, because I had documentation that represented the facts. Perhaps, had she not sought to embarrass me in public, I wouldn't have been so compelled to defend my honor publicly. If history was any indicator, she knew that she could count on me, and everyone else, to accept her unwarranted wrath.

I had always thought that, as long as I did my job with excellence or to the best of my ability, in return—at the very least—I could count on mutual respect. Life was teaching me a new set of rules. My nerves were, simply put, a wreck. I felt safe going to human resources, because anyone who knew my boss had to know that I was telling the truth.

Although I was assured that my confidence would be kept, the very next day, I was fired.

It took years to recover from the emotional impact of the Freddie Mac experience However, now I am so much stronger, wiser and better because of it.

Because my ADD medicine was beginning to transform me with a different way of thinking and behaving, it required quite an adjustment, under the best of circumstances. The disruption in my life left me no other option but to return to what was familiar and abandon my medicine.

Several years later, I had the courage to go back on medication, and although I still struggle, I am enjoying the person that I have become. Even out of ashes, the sun rises. For without the Freddie Mac experience, I would never have confronted the reality of my disability and accepted responsibility for it. While it was tough going through that kind of rejection, humiliation, and threat to my family's livelihood at the Freddie Mac Foundation, it was perhaps the most transforming event in my adult life. The experience taught me that living a wholesome life meant learning how to treat both triumph and disaster the same. I have been strengthened by that.

I once believed that the commitment of the Freddie Mac Foundation to children was unwavering. Nothing that was done to me can change my appreciation for the fact that the Freddie Mac Foundation has made substantial contributions in many ways to children, youth, and families—both before and during the tenure of my former boss.

You can't imagine how vindicating it was when, several years after my leaving the foundation, an extensive article was published in the

Washington Post, discussing an external agency's investigation into allegations that the CEO of the foundation subjected staff members to unfair employment practices. The allegations reported in the newspaper mirrored the confidential complaints I had shared with the human resources department and which they had subsequently leaked to my boss the day before I was unjustly fired.

I couldn't help but feel sad for those remaining in that environment. I had always thought that, as long as I did my job with excellence or to the best of my ability, in return—at the very least—I could count on mutual respect.

I hope the atmosphere has improved and has since become a safe, healthy place for people to serve children without the threat of misplaced egos or vendettas.

I take great comfort and pride in some of the Freddie Mac Foundation's accomplishments while I was its director of foundation giving. Primarily, we gave support to the Congressional Coalition on Adoption during its formative stages, which was cochaired by Senators Mary Landrieu (D/LA) and Larry Craig (R/ID) at that time. Under their leadership and with support from many others, the coalition ultimately launched the Congressional Coalition on Adoption Institute (CCAI), a nonprofit, nonpartisan organization that is dedicated to raising awareness about the tens of thousands of foster children in this country, as well as the millions of orphans around the world in need of permanent, safe, and loving homes. CCAI also attempts to eliminate the barriers that keep those children from becoming part of families.

The Angels in Adoption Program is CCAI's signature public awareness program. Every year, CCAI invites all members of Congress to select—from their home state—an individual, family, or organization that has significantly contributed to changing the lives of children in need through adoption and foster care. Both the "Angels" and the member of Congress who selected them attend the annual Angels in Adoption Awards Gala, where they meet and share their personal experiences. Congressional directors of CCAI also select "National Angels," honoring recipients for their nationwide and international work. If you know of an unsung hero who is making a difference in the life of a child, contact the congressional representative of that district to initiate the nomination process for this distinguished award.

I am equally proud of another initiative—the support we gave to the Oliver Project through the Orphan Foundation. In 1981, the late Joseph Rivers, a former foster youth from the Syracuse area, started the Orphan Foundation of America (OFA). His goal was simple: to help orphans and foster youth as they transition from foster care to young adulthood, with particular emphasis on helping those young men and women attend college and vocational school. Twenty years later, his dream is alive and well. Through the leadership of his foster sister Eileen McCaffrey, a woman for whom I have tremendous respect and who continues to passionately champion his vision, OFA truly raises national awareness of foster care issues and the comprehensive services needed for older youth. I've witnessed firsthand the effect that OFA and its scholarship partners have had on vulnerable survivors of foster care; those organizations provide a much-needed safety net for foster children pursuing postsecondary education.

You know you are doing something right when you attract both (former) Representative Tom Delay (R/TX) and (former) Senator Hillary Clinton (D/NY) as committed supporters. Both politicians have supported the organization and attended the Orphan Foundation's Celebration of Excellence dinner. Creating adequate services for older youth in the foster care system is an issue that requires collaboration and a nonpartisan approach. Only that spirit of cooperation and determination will help the United States realize the full potential of our children and make us the great nation we are capable of being.

In 2000, while still shell-shocked from the Freddie Mac Foundation experience, I was asked to serve as the chief of staff to the deputy mayor for Children, Youth, Families, and Elders of the District of Columbia. I consulted with William Bell, who had just become the commissioner of New York's foster care system, before accepting the position. He said that, as chief of staff, I would learn more in six months than I would in many years at any other place. That comment sealed it for me.

What an awesome growth opportunity and professional challenge it was! Every day, I learned something new. One of the benchmarks of success that I set for myself was to respond to the complex and competing constituent needs so well that there would be no way that the press could use my name to embarrass Mayor Anthony Williams, himself the product of the foster care system. It certainly wasn't easy, given the agencies for which we had oversight responsibility—including the Department of Health, Child, and Family Services Administration;

the Department of Human Services; the Office of Human Rights; the Office of Aging; the Department of Parks and Recreation; the State Education Office; and the Public Library System. Our agency administered the largest percentage of the city's budget, and our plates were full. It was an incredible experience and quite a roller-coaster ride.

The mayor was brilliant, and like many graduates of the foster care system, was often underestimated. I related to him, admired him, felt vested in his success, and was proud to serve in an administration that was filled with incredible talent and committed to the renaissance of the nation's capital. Not even in my wildest dreams had I envisioned such a role for myself. Despite everything, I'd come a long way.

Even more rewarding, however, was serving with Deputy Mayor Carolyn Graham, who was passionate and determined to achieve gains for children in the District of Columbia.

The Council for Court Excellence found that the city's ability to reach decisions in child neglect and abuse cases and to meet the Adoption and Safe Families Act (ASFA) deadlines improved steadily, particularly in cases where children had been removed from their homes.

What gave me the greatest satisfaction was the city's implementation of the Family Drug Treatment Court. If my mother had had access to a similar program, I am certain our story would have had a better outcome. Modeled after similar programs in New York, Florida, Ohio, and Virginia, the program gives mothers a chance to rebuild their lives and their families within ASFA time lines. Mothers who qualify for the program are permitted to live with their children at a treatment facility while undergoing six months of rigorous, supervised drug treatment. In addition, the women receive job training and classes in managing a household, budgeting, and parenting. At the end of that time, they enter a six-month aftercare program. One of the most significant advantages of the program is that it enables children to stay out of foster care and remain with their mothers.

What a long way we have come ... in just my lifetime! Sometimes, it is hard for me to believe it when I think about what was not available to my family but what is now available to other families. Yet, I am acutely aware of how great the need still is. We need more treatment facilities like the one I just described. Can you imagine the positive effect and overall cost savings if we invested nationwide in programs designed to ensure that families remained together? It's not only the right thing to do, but it is also less of a burden on taxpayers.

In 2002, the deputy mayor resigned, which meant that, as her chief of staff and a political appointee, I was resigning with her. I had no clue what I would do next. Then a call came from the Board of Directors at CASA (Court-Appointed Special Advocates) of DC, an organization I had helped start before going to the mayor's office. Sadly, the executive director had just had a stroke. I agreed to serve as the interim executive director while I thought through my long-term options. There was no way I could say no. I believed in the mission of the organization and happened to be available. I did not expect to stay beyond the interim period, but once I started working there, I realized it was a perfect fit. That position was my calling. It was clear that I was supposed to return and finish what I had begun. I could motivate Washingtonians to support and help find permanent homes for the 2,800 children in DC's child welfare system.

I knew that CASA was one of the best-kept secret solutions for moving children through the child welfare system quickly and safely. The grassroots, DC organization was searching for visionary leadership to engage the community in finding permanent and safe homes for abused or neglected children. Because I strongly believe that each of us holds a key to unlock the door to a child's heart, community activism was a challenge that I was prepared to accept.

My one question was determining whether I could live on a nonprofit salary with seven children. Gloria and I struggled with that problem and ultimately found a salary figure that would fit the organization's budget yet would not have a devastating effect on our family. It was liberating to not make money the issue.

Everything in my life had prepared me for this opportunity to lead. I had to be true to myself by being true to others. I was stepping out in faith, and I have never regretted my decision. The staff, volunteers, and board of CASA for Children of DC have made tremendous strides. I pursue funding from every viable source so that the citizens of the Washington metropolitan area can volunteer as advocates and give children hope.

Chapter 13
YOU GOTTA BE STRONGER

You gotta be bad, you gotta be bold, you gotta be wiser,
You gotta be hard, you gotta be tough, you gotta be stronger,
You gotta be cool, you gotta be calm, you gotta stay together
All I know, All I know is love will save the day.
—Des'ree

I began my job with the government of the District of Columbia living in Ashburn, Virginia, though; the commute of an hour to an hour and a half from Ashburn to DC quickly became impossible for me. My attention deficit disorder couldn't sit in traffic every morning and afternoon without going wild, so I took a tiny apartment on Capitol Hill. I lived in the district during the week and went back out to Ashburn on Friday night, returning on Monday morning.

Being by myself for a few days a week brought changes. After running myself ragged for years and never giving myself time to think, I realized that I had to confront my pain and look at and listen to myself, so I could learn who I really was. Initially, I had thought that, because I hadn't turned out too badly, the system must have been okay, with a few hiccups here and there. It wasn't until I started engaging in dialogue with my grown daughter, Tiffany, learning from my other children, and looking at the relationships I'd been unable to sustain, both personally and professionally over the course of my life, that I realized the price I had paid for all those years of abandonment, rejection, abuse, and neglect.

As an adult, I had assured myself that I knew what love was and that I was giving it to those who mattered to me most. However, as I

135

went through this process of self-reflection, I began to realize that I was repeating the cycle of neglect and abuse—emotionally, if not physically. All my life, I'd fought to not abandon Tiffany—to not do to her what had been done to me. To me, success meant I did not physically abandon her or walk out on her the way my parents had walked out on me, but I was so *busy* providing the home and family I thought Tiffany deserved that I was an emotionally absent father. During one of our talks, she looked at me and said, in a way that wrenched my heart, "Dad, don't you realize all I ever needed was you?"

I had always tried to do the right thing. When it became clear that her birth mother was not going to step up to the plate, I had gotten her the best mom on the planet, my wife Gloria. I thought Tiffany should have siblings to support her through life's struggles when she grew up, so we had adopted other children and had some of our own, creating a large family whose members could help each other in hard times and celebrate together in good times. Because I wanted to make sure that all the children received a good public education, I had moved the family into a neighborhood in one of the best school districts in the area. But to maintain this large family in a good area, I had had to take demanding jobs with long hours. Between working to assure that my children would not have the negative experience that I had had and fulfilling my desire to change the plight of other faceless American children in foster care, I had burned myself out and become emotionally drained. My kids got an emotional blank check from me, even though it was signed "with love." I had had the best of intentions, but my execution wasn't enough.

Somewhere along the line, everything had become about the mechanics of love and not about love itself. I had received training on real intimacy and good parenting, and I understood them intellectually, but in reality, I ran from both of them. No matter how many people I had around me, I felt isolated and lonely.

I think one of the biggest challenges faced by many abused or neglected children is dealing with social and interpersonal relationships, which has certainly been my greatest challenge. As much as I love my family and as proud as I am of my life, I wish I could have learned as a young adult the skills that I would need later in life to create healthy intimacies and to resolve conflicts.

I am lucky that I was able to bond with my mother during the first four years of my life. Many abandoned kids, including my own brother Keith, never get the chance to bond with anyone, and that lack affects them deeply. Bonding; learning to trust; learning what you truly like and dislike; learning to recognize what you want and then how to ask for it; learning to say no and set boundaries; learning to be yourself and to stop wearing masks all the time—these are things children must learn how to do before they can become healthy adults.

Resolving conflict is also a challenge for many abused or abandoned kids, particularly those in foster care. If your environment changes every time the going gets tough, how do you ever learn to work things out? Of course, the adults you live with have to be willing to work things out with you as well. As you can tell from reading earlier chapters in this book, some of the adults in my life could do this, and some couldn't. And there wasn't anything I could do about that then.

But I *can* do something about it now. As an adult, I can choose the people who are part of my life. In addition to developing conflict resolution skills, I have learned how to let go of people who are toxic and unwilling to love me for me. Both of those abilities have made a big difference in my life.

Because I had to depend on myself when I was young, I didn't know how to depend on others. I gave and gave. I didn't know how to receive and would wallow in disappointment when my needs weren't met. I was caught in a vicious cycle, unable to let people give me what I needed, unable to feel that I ever fit in. Being with people became more and more of a burden.

When I was younger, I had never asked myself what *I* wanted, what *I* needed, or what was right for *me*. First, I had focused on what my foster parents wanted, and later, I had focused on making sure that Tiffany and the rest of my family had what they wanted. I thought that happiness rested on pleasing others and on meeting or exceeding expectations. Because of that belief, after Tiffany graduated, joined the Navy, and was on her own, I felt that the expectations I had set for myself when she was born had been met.

I began falling apart when she left, almost like a mother with empty-nest syndrome, except my nest wasn't empty. My nest still had plenty of children in it and a beautiful wife whom I was not treating as a partner. I had been consumed by being a patriarch, and I had nothing left. I couldn't be a lover, a husband, a father, or even just plain Shane.

I didn't have any of the skills I needed to be a real person without the masks and the roles and the demands that had filled my life. Those facades were my life.

The idea of being totally alone in a room was terrifying, but I realized that solitude was what I needed to enable me to discover and embrace myself. So I moved into my DC apartment full-time. Although we continued to function as a family, I did not live with Gloria and the children for several years. I chose for the first time in my life to live alone and face my demons. I struggled to work through my issues with hopes of becoming the best man I could be, but only now in my forties, am I learning who I really am, how to love myself, and how to let other people love me as well. Grandma and Gloria gave me the love and support I needed to start my journey of healing, but I learned that I needed to be alone, at least temporarily, to complete it, that I had nothing to give to anyone until I got the basics under my belt. It has taken me almost a lifetime to realize that you must be grounded in a comprehensive understanding of yourself, truth, and God's love before your foundation is rock solid; what grows from that solid foundation can't be shaken. It was time to grow up inside and stop acting like the foster child in a new home and wearing my mask with the hope that people would like me enough to keep me. I started looking at my difficulties one by one. It was a challenge, but I needed to be hard, tough, and stronger.

Listening to others has always been a challenge for me. I catch myself interrupting other people before they have completed their thoughts. For a long time, I wasn't aware of how often I did this, how annoying it is, or how I looked to others. I just knew that people seemed to shut down after they talked with me for a while. I came to realize that this habit was out of fear of being still, close, and silent with people. Ever since I can remember, I've been afraid of silence. It was very silent when my mother left, and I never wanted to hear that again.

Another aspect of my interpersonal challenge stems from my ADD. It isn't unusual for me to get distracted during conversations and then start rambling, moving way beyond the initial point I intended to make. Because I've had ADD all my life, I believed that the disrupted thoughts and the associated behavior—which have had devastating effects on my relationships and on how people perceive me—were my burden alone.

Only recently have I learned, through group therapy, that ADD has played a bigger role than I first suspected in making me feel so disconnected from others. There is so much more to the condition than what most of us hear in sound bites. The image of ADD, often interchanged with ADHD (attention deficit/hyperactivity disorder), is of a hot-wired kid bouncing off the walls. But the reality is that many people with ADD feel so different that they don't know how to connect with people, and at some point, they just stop trying. Many of us medicate the pain, which results in addictions of some kind. I'm overcoming mine.

My extreme passion in conveying my thoughts or carrying out actions has also been misconstrued. I hadn't realized that this intensity could, at times, come across as arrogance or insensitivity. When I slip into hyper-focus (another manifestation of ADD), some think I'm being self-absorbed. Realizing that I was missing key social cues increased my belief that I was just screwed up.

I had shared the pain of my isolation only with my grandmother. She was the one who saw how hard it was for me to overcome the lingering effects of abandonment and to build meaningful personal relationships.

I had survived by putting on different masks so I could give people whatever impression was necessary to be granted opportunities and to be a welcome presence in their lives. Whenever I tried to show my true self, I often lost friends and even loved ones, who couldn't figure out whether I was Dr. Jekyll or Mr. Hyde and who would cut bait and run. To shield myself from the heartbreaks associated with rejection and disappointment, I built intricate defense mechanisms, locking up my intimate emotions in separate boxes.

Grandma knew all about those boxes—she had some of her own and was trying to break through them too, which was what gave her permission to look into my soul. I'm still working on finding the keys to my boxes, so I can open them and let in all the people I love.

I'm also trying to drop my masks with my children, to be fully present and engaged in my relationships with them, to experience the beauty of their spirits, and to invite them to do the same with me. I aspire to be a whole person with them. Up until now, I've been able to share only a part of myself with my family. At home, I have been the provider and protector—two roles I'm good at. I've played those roles since the age of four.

However, I've been afraid to be still and enjoy the moment. To this day, I dread intimate "quality" moments. This inability to open up has hurt Gloria and my children, but especially Gloria. She has been there for me 100 percent, even though I wouldn't let her come really close and wouldn't be as close to her as she needed in return. Somehow, she has always loved me anyway.

I'm sharing all these personal revelations to let people know that wanting to break the cycle of generational demons is the first step, but it's not enough. Hope rides on learning *how* to do it, and you start that learning by making an honest inventory of your strengths and your weaknesses. Once you see where the gaps are in your life, you can find hope on this journey to the dream with your name on it.

When you escape your own prison, when you let yourself become free of your past and embark on the road to healing your broken spirit, then you are able to truly create a different future for yourself and for the people who want to love you. I am learning how to ask for help whenever I need it, and I will keep asking and trying until I am whole.

My family and I relocated to Washington, DC to start our road to healing. I guess sometimes scars are just too deep and masks have to come off eventually. After four years of effort, Gloria and I separated as friends with a steadfast commitment to our children. This most recent change in my life leaves me unable to fully express the complexity of my feelings.

My family was all I ever knew and now a world waits for me in a house without them. I choose to embrace this part of my journey not as a sad ending but rather a new beginning for now.

Chapter 14

FIRE AND RAIN

I've seen fire, and I've seen rain.
I've seen sunny days that I thought would never end;
I've seen lonely times when I could not find a friend;
But I always thought I'd see you again.
—James Taylor

I remember tender, innocent feelings that I used to have as a little boy, and I remember when I lost them. While I can never make the pain that gets in the way of my intimate relationships go away completely, I can certainly keep working on my day-to-day efforts to manage it. My sole focus at this stage of my life is on learning who I am and how to love me—no more pretending to be what I'm not, no more pushing who I am aside. So forgive me, when you meet me, if you find that I talk a little too much, or if I walk a little too fast, fight a little too hard, and choose to keep company with the underdogs. I'm just a plain ol' guy, who's a work in progress, who says what he means and means what he says. Misunderstood and disliked by many and loved by a few, the only way I can truly love my family and others who are important to me is to first know, accept, and love myself.

My grandmother opened this door of hope for me on the day she rocked me in her arms, laid my head on her lap, and simply said, "I know, baby, I know." She had known that, all of my life, I had just wanted to know what love felt like. I had longed to be wanted, understood, and connected—something I lost early, something that all the moving from home to home had taken away from me.

When Grandma said, "I know, baby, I know," I couldn't believe she really did know until I learned her story. Then I suddenly realized that her story was my story, and my pain was our common understanding. Light bulbs started flashing as I looked into her eyes and saw all the years of heartache, disappointment, and broken dreams riding heavily on her back.

Grandma's pain had become her poison, and she had been imprisoned by it. But the gates opened for both of us, and our opportunity for healing unfolded. I opened my heart wide, and love came dancing into my soul for the very first time. She struggled, trying to give what she thought was love to her children only to realize that in so many ways what she gave was not what they needed most. Until recently, I was doing the same thing. Fortunately, I have the chance to continue working on the path to healing and recovery. Grandma doesn't.

My grandmother died on Christmas Eve a few years ago. She was taken to a hospital in New York, where they found a malignancy on her kidney. For reasons I never did understand, her daughter, Jewel, didn't want me there and encouraged others in the family not to call me. However, Grandma's best friend, Linda, knowing that my grandmother would want to see me, did call us, although not until it was too late. Gloria took the call (I was at a shopping mall) and got the sad news that Grandma wasn't doing well.

"She's been in the hospital all weekend," Linda told my wife. "She's tired after the surgery just last month, and I think she's really ready to go."

"What do you mean?" Gloria asked in disbelief. "How could she just give up?"

"I'm telling you, it doesn't look good," came the reply. "She asked for papers about no more procedures or something like that. A whole bunch of doctors then came into the room, asking her all kinds of questions. 'What's your name? Who's the president? What year is it?' Know what I mean?"

"Yes," said Gloria, who understood that the doctors were trying to determine if she was of sound mind when she refused further intervention by signing an order not to resuscitate.

"Even after they told her she would be dead in hours if she didn't go on dialysis," continued Linda, "she said no. Shane has to get here. I wasn't supposed to call him, because of you-know-who, but that ain't right, and I just couldn't let this go down like that."

While thanking Linda and telling her how grateful I would be for her call, Gloria started to sob. It had been only a few years since her adoptive mother had died—by a strange coincidence also around Christmas—and Grandma had been her strength, helping her through it, tiptoeing around, but keeping a watchful eye. Gloria just couldn't believe that our family was facing another devastating loss after such a short time. She remembered all the good times she had shared with Grandma over the years—their private talks and their soap opera updates.

Brittney and Courtney came downstairs and saw Gloria weeping. Brittney, our nurturing child, immediately asked what was wrong. As Gloria asked them to sit down, Courtney, our child who says whatever comes to mind, blurted out, "Did someone die or something?" Little did she know how close to the truth her perception was. When Gloria told them that Grandma Salter was in the hospital and was not going to make it, they couldn't believe it at first.

Brittney, in dismay, mentioned that she was going to miss Grandma's cooking.

Courtney followed, saying she would miss Grandma's infamous one-liners. And then she started quoting them:

"You'd have to be Ray Charles not to see that," which she'd say when someone tried to pull a fast one.

"Leave this old lady alone; I'm not losing any weight. Let me tell you: don't nobody want a bone but a dog!" (When I urged her to lose weight.)

"Give me my flowers while I'm here, not when there's a tag on my toe." (About postponing love, reward, or praise.)

"This family is dysfunctional with a capital D!" (Whenever someone did something crazy in New York.)

Gloria called me on my cell phone and told me about Grandma's condition. I sprinted for the train station. I could barely see straight. On the train, my phone rang again. It was Jewel, informing me that Grandma had gone "peacefully with everyone by her bedside as she took her final breath."

Everyone except me, I thought. All I could do was moan and cry out, "No, no, no."

"Trust me; it was beautiful, Shane," Jewel said. "She was ready to go home. She left with a smile like she saw something, and her last word—I couldn't believe it—was 'Hallelujah!'"

I felt like she was rubbing in the fact that I had missed being there, like it was a call meant to convey spite more than anything else. Since then, I've tried to come to terms with that sad experience by rationalizing that Jewel and the others may have needed that time with Grandma more than I did.

I often teased Grandma by begging her not to leave me behind to deal with her daughter's drama and the rest of the family when she died. However, I meant it when I told her, "If you happen to leave first, count on the fact that, after I put your remains in the ground, the relationships I have with the rest of this family will be buried as well. I won't let them do to me what they've done to you." She heard me quietly, and—although, I know she did not agree—she certainly understood.

Because our relationship had been so close, I was sure that, during her final hours and at her funeral, I wouldn't feel like an outsider from foster care. Yet, the way my family in New York treated me sent a powerful message and almost made me feel that way again. I knew Gloria and all of my children were grieving, especially David, who was very close to Grandma himself. I focused on the goal and remained strong for everyone.

When I arrived at the hospital in the Bronx, I learned that Grandma's body had already been taken down to the morgue. I told them I was the executor and asked to be taken to the morgue to say good-bye. I wasn't sure that I was really ready, but I felt calm, as if she and I were doing this thing together. I walked in and saw my grandmother's body, her skin smooth as silk. At first, I just stared.

Then the orderly said, as he left to give me privacy, "I've never seen a body this peaceful down here; she has no hint of strain or stress on her face."

I stroked Grandma's cheek. It was a little cold, but not so cold that I couldn't tell that it was only recently that she had departed on her journey home. While I was sad that she was gone, I was happy to see her at peace. It was clear to me that the pain and heartache that had consumed her while she lived were over. Her tasks were done, and she appeared to be at rest.

I simply said to her, "Now you can get the peace you were unable to find here on earth. Just tell my mother for me that I love her and miss her love every day. I don't know how I will get through this, Ma. I don't know how I will go on without you. Who will I turn to when I need to talk late at night? Who will I call from the car during those long drives to and from home, burning countless cell phone minutes? No one understood me like you did."

And then I made her a promise: "Ma, I will get through this. I will be strong, and I will be patient with Jewel. I'll hold my tongue until this is over and be strong for Pierre too.

"Thank you for loving me," I added. "Thank you for showing me what love *really* is. Thank you for believing I could do anything, even when I thought otherwise."

I then kissed her gently on the forehead one last time and said good-bye. I like to think she felt that kiss.

My grandmother had been my strength and my pride; she had helped take my loneliness away. Now, like all the others who had journeyed down this road and suffered this kind of loss, I had to find a way to survive. But that's where my faith came in. I knew I would make it, because God promises that, although weeping may endure for a night, joy will come in the morning.

Because it was Christmas and no arrangements could be made for a few days, I got on Amtrak and went back to DC in a daze. While I was on the train, I remembered that everything in my life happened for a reason, and I decided that my grandma had probably arranged it so that she and I had our private time for closure just the way it had played out. We had created a very special relationship, and it had ended in a very special way that was just for us. However, I couldn't help but also think that this was going to be yet another miserable holiday season. Gloria's mom had died December 9; my mother had died December 16; and Robbie and my grandmother had died December 24. How do you ever experience a happy Christmas again with those kinds of losses during the holidays?

When I returned home, I anxiously tried to track down Keith. Finally, I found Ma Mills in Richmond at her daughter Joni's house, and she agreed to relay the news to Keith.

But I still had not come to terms with Grandma's death.

Alone in my Capitol Hill apartment, the reality was beginning to hit me—my grandmother and best friend was really gone. I lost my appetite, I couldn't sleep, and I couldn't keep still. I wasn't able to let Gloria and the kids help me, and my best male friend was away for Christmas. Luckily, my other friend Reese stopped by. He quickly realized what a hard time I was having, that I couldn't seem to jump-start my usual family patriarch role, and that I couldn't start any task related to planning Grandma's funeral. Reese called around, got help, and carried me through it. We sat together and planned Grandma's service according to her expressed wishes.

Ironically, the only other time I had been that vulnerable and in that much pain was when I lost my job at the Freddie Mac Foundation on Grandma's birthday. The big difference was that Grandma was there to see me through it and to remind me that I'd been through rough seas and crossed too many bridges to let myself think my ship was going to sink now. This time I had to trust that, in my time of need, I wouldn't be left hanging. I always knew that Grandma would not walk away, and if I stumbled, grown man or not, she would be there to catch me and to keep me from hitting the ground. This time, I would have to work through things the best way I knew how—in silence and alone. Perhaps having had Grandma's support through the pain, rejection, and humiliation when I lost my job had prepared me for what I would eventually call a one-two-three punch.

I went back up to New York and finished the rest of the arrangements. There, Pierre let me know he would not be coming to his mother's funeral. When I asked him why, he said that he couldn't stand being in the same space as his sister. He came to the funeral home and said good-bye to his mother before the service; then he left. It was a shame, but I accepted his wishes.

It was frustrating that all of those loving family members who had cried and carried on at her bedside were not around to help then. Only my sister Shanique and my cousin Omar (who had also been shunned by the family during Grandma's final hours) were brave enough to accompany me as I tried to deal with Jewel and to arrange Grandma's funeral.

The only experience that I recall fearing more was going through the gas chamber during basic training in the US Navy. Just as then, my eyes were full of tears, barely was I able to breathe, and overwhelming was the fear that I would never make it through to see the sun again. I struggled to balance my grieving spirit, having lost the woman whose life had helped me, through forgiveness and reconciliation, discover freedom from the prison of my pain and managing my conflicted feelings with an aunt that I had grown to despise.

I was committed to ensuring the noneventful funeral service my grandmother deserved. And that meant going out of my way to be kind to Jewel, even driving her back and forth in my car. To help increase my tolerance level and manage my temperament, I planned what I believe to be an authentic memorial service for Grandma. This one was at our family church outside of DC in Reston, Virginia, where she had occasionally visited. That way, no matter what went down in New York, I knew that Grandma would have a spirit-filled, drama-free tribute.

The morning of the funeral felt like a day I had dreaded all of my life. I wanted to get through it as quickly as possible. We were all afraid that Jewel would make a scene, so Shanique and I walked next to her, each of us holding one of her hands. Gloria and the children were right behind me. Jewel didn't make a scene—but then she had already struck.

Before the service even began, Jewel had stolen the silver plate inscribed with Grandma's name out of the coffin.

When I pointed it out to Shanique, my sister said, loudly enough for everyone to hear, "Unbelievable. Stealing out of the coffin! Unbelievable. Robbing the dead. I've seen it all." Although I too was disgusted by Jewel's action, my sister's uncontrolled outburst almost caused me to burst out laughing.

All I could do was pray, "Dear Lord, just get me through this." My worst fear was that a fight would break out, someone would knock over Grandma's casket, her body would roll out of the church onto the street, and hair weaves would fly everywhere—the makings of a Salter made-for-TV movie directed by Spike Lee, for sure. I wonder what we would have called it.

We got through the service without any more drama, thank goodness.

Planning the funeral, riding in the limousine directly behind the hearse, and being my Grandma's executor somehow erased all the leftover pain from the rejection and abandonment I had experienced in my childhood. Through forgiveness and reconciliation, I had found the hope that, one day, Grandma would accept, love, and appreciate me. That hope fueled my journey to what became the dream with my name on it. I found closure for everything that had been denied me at my mother's death. I no longer felt illegitimate. Knowing that, when we arrived at the cemetery, I would be the one to sign the papers authorizing the plot to be opened, there was no denying my legitimacy. I was the family patriarch, and the only one to whom Grandma could entrust her final arrangements. This was my family, for better or worse. No longer did I have to try on someone else's last name or change my first name in search of a new identity.

I am a Salter—Shane Lenard Rico Salter Sr.—the great-grandson of Richard Sawyer; the first grandchild of Sandra Ethelyn Sawyer-Salter; the first son of Sharon Elaine Salter; and the father of David Lenard, Tiffany Monique, Shane Rico, Brittney Nicole, Courtney Shanade, Moyé Jordan, and Nigel Keith. My great-grandfather, my grandmother, and my mother were the people whose living gave me my life, my history, and the strength to become who I am today.

As I looked over Grandma's coffin, I believed that she was finally at rest, and I understood that my task was almost complete. My final expression of love was to escort her body to the cemetery without the conflict and drama that had plagued our family for generations. As Grandma had requested, the procession of limousines and cars followed the hearse to Fairlawn Cemetery, where she would join Uncle Leroy and my mother.

As I got out of the limousine, many people were there, but my misty eyes stopped me from seeing them clearly. Tremors caused my cold hands to shake uncontrollably. I could not bear to see the sadness in the faces of my wife and children as we gathered at the gravesite. The grave handlers asked if I wanted to watch the lowering of the coffin. Without hesitation, I said yes. I couldn't help but look into the grave and try to see my mother's coffin; this was the closest I had been to her since I was four years old. A part of me wanted to jump into the grave and put my arms around the box that held her remains.

I still mourn and ache for my mother. All of my life, I had tried everything to fill the gaping hole that her absence had left in my heart. Its depth was mirrored only by the size of this gravesite. The one who had helped me fill that hole was about to fill the one before me. My grandmother was the first person I had learned to love authentically, and I was watching her coffin be lowered on top of the coffin occupied by the body of the woman I had longed every waking day to see again, the one who gave me life.

When the funeral director and minister were done, I hugged various family members as we all walked to cars and designated limousines. My driver knew the plan. The limousine that Gloria, the kids, and I had ridden in was going back empty to New York. My son David had driven the family up from Virginia in our SUV and had followed the processional to the cemetery in New Jersey.

I wanted to leave for Washington straight from the cemetery and not spend one minute more than necessary with the toxic members of Grandma's family. Once she was in the ground, we jumped in the Yukon and headed for home. I left the cemetery and never looked back, just as I had told Grandma I would.

Shortly after we got onto the New Jersey Turnpike and with David at the wheel, I opened the letter my grandmother had left for me in the box with her burial papers. I had distributed the letters she had left for other members of the family as instructed, but I had waited to read mine until the service was over.

We had often talked about death, and Grandma and I had always agreed that, when either of us went, there should be no "boo-hooing" or "falling out" over the casket, because all of our love had been expressed while we lived. We never let a conversation end without saying "I love you" or a visit end without a big, mushy hug and kiss. We laughed and told each other everything, so that was supposed to be enough to get me through all of this. But I should have known that Grandma would somehow find a way to have the last word.

Hi Darling:

I know that this is a sad time for you. You know, baby, that you are my first grandchild, my best friend; we could talk and say anything to each other. I love you and have loved you more than you will ever know, but you have known that. You know that you are my baby, and you have given me so much joy. You have made me so proud of you. Also, you gave me my flowers when I was around, all the time; never was there ever anything that you thought I wanted or needed that you didn't make possible. Shane, I love you so much. I haven't left you; just look, and you will see me smile. One day, we will be together again. I will always be around you. The bond is there, and it always will be.

When you play that song, "Precious Lord," think of me; think of me when you made me laugh, when you said silly things to me. Be strong; take care of yourself and family. I love you so much.

Love you,
"Mom"

Although my wounds are deep, and evidence of scarring will always exist, there is no amount of money or inherited material possessions that could have brought me the comfort and peace of mind that her last letter did.

When she first started coming to visit me, Grandma did not attend a church, and her faith was weak, to say the least. Through our relationship with Gloria and the family, she also developed a relationship with our pastor, attended church regularly, and clearly asked in her final hours of life for God to forgive her for any wrong she had ever done. I was so glad to hear that my grandmother's last word was "Hallelujah!" Because we had a relationship rooted in forgiveness and reconciliation, we both experienced a spiritual transformation. I refused to give up hope that someday I would have a family and live the dream that I believed had my name on it.

Chapter 15
WHERE ARE THEY NOW?

Keith and I don't have much of a relationship. It's unfortunate; we were inseparable as kids, until he was twelve, and I was fifteen. Now, we are more like Cain and Abel. After numerous failed attempts to work out our problems, I've let him go. Our bond has fallen victim to our experience, but who knows what could happen in the future. I respect him for all that he has endured and accomplished and for fighting the good fight.

My sister, Shanique, lives in New York with her beautiful son, my nephew Shalik. Since my grandmother's funeral, we have not really talked much, other than an occasional birthday call. That doesn't change the fact that I continue to be so proud of the woman she's become and the great mother she turned out to be.

My brother, David, went to technical school and became a certified cable installer. David has worked for Verizon for more than six years. He and his wife own their own home in Maryland. I can't help but chuckle as I watch him repeatedly open his doors to relatives and friends down on their luck—a chip off the old block, if I do say so myself. Unfortunately, three months after Grandma was buried, David was involved in a tragic, head-on collision. The threat of losing my brother right after my grandmother almost pushed me off the deep end. It was touch-and-go for a while, but David has recovered well.

My oldest son, David, serves in the army national guard, works for the federal government, and lives outside of Richmond, Virginia. He has a healthy relationship with his birth father and sisters, along with his former foster father.

Tiffany, my firstborn, has accepted her mother's limited capacity to deliver on promises and to fully engage with her in a nourishing relationship. However, the pain has manifested in ways I could never have imagined. As expressed in a rap CD she recorded and gave to me, Tiffany recognizes how much it took as a teen father to step up to the plate, remain there, and ensure that her needs were met. As a result, our relationship is rooted in forgiveness, and we love each other unconditionally.

Shane Rico, my first son through adoption, lives in his New York apartment not far from Tiffany. He has settled down in a serious relationship and recently became a daddy. Well, I guess that means I also became a granddaddy—Grandpapa? Gramps? Oh no! I never imagined this. Shane enjoys information technology, and through careful supervision over the past few years, he has transitioned off all medication.

I am really thrilled that the bond between Moyé and Nigel appears to be impenetrable. They are extremely close and are progressing well, both in school and socially.

Brittney and Courtney have both evolved into wonderful young ladies. Brittney recently graduated from high school and is considering a career in the military. Courtney is pursuing her career as a singer, having recently signed with an independent record label.

Tara, Tiffany's mom, raised her children in South Carolina. Her sons were returned from emergency foster care several years ago and, as I understand, have begun to present with challenging issues against authority.

Aunt Cookie's son, Omar, is working in Washington, DC. He is a wonderful, committed father of four children and an inspiration to his brother and sister.

The Moragnes, my unofficial foster parents, have retired and now live in Greenwood, South Carolina. Dad Moragne survived a major heart attack a few years ago. I took that occasion during his recovery to make sure to remind him of how he had inspired me to share this journey with the public as an opportunity for learning and healing. It was Dad Moragne who had thought that, after all I had gone through, just graduating from high school alone was a miracle. Anything else I would go on to achieve after that was certainly a testament to the purpose my life was destined to serve for others.

He told me, "You're supposed to do something with all of this. Write it down. People need to know about it what you endured to get where you are."

I never thought much of the struggle quite frankly. It was just a fact of life, but although I was only seventeen when he said those words, I promised him that I would write this book some day, and now that promise is fulfilled.

Reverend Cameron relocated to Washington and continues to love and adopt more children. Dad Cameron is one of the few people I had the great opportunity to reconcile with through forgiveness, and he now plays an active role in my life as friend, dad, and as grandpa to my children. We have a great adult relationship. He is a complex, yet straightforward person. I understand him much better now, and I love him for his heart and the sincerity of his intentions. What we were unable to have when I was a kid, we are enjoying twofold as adults.

I never saw Mr. Pointer again. I have searched for him. People I've met on the lecture circuit have also offered to search for him in all kinds of creative ways. After all the heartache I caused him and all the time he invested in me, I wish he could have seen the man I've become. He was a powerful social worker with a profound effect on my life.

As much as I had hoped that Ma Jenkins and me would be able to rebuild our relationship, after Dad died, it was less than a year before her health began to rapidly deteriorate. I only learned of her failing health upon notice of the death of her last surviving sister, Aunt Emma. When I arrived for Aunt Emma's funeral, I was met at the door and warned about Mom's condition. While attempts were made by the family to be respectful and sensitive—you might say—there was no getting around the elephant in the room.

I may not have known of Mom's condition if it had not been for the death of her sister. The rapid decline in Mom's health ultimately required that she be placed in a nursing home. It was in that facility that I received my closure. That year as she lay in that hospital bed, I was given my opportunity to visit every other week without her capacity to utter any harsh words or impose rejection.

Consequently, I seized the moment to say all that I could never say in a card, in a telephone call, or through flowers. I just wanted her to know that I had tried to be the best son I could be. On one pivotal visit, I had fallen to my knees, and I could barely see straight because my eyes were swollen from crying. It was greater than me—it must have been spiritual or something—but whatever the reason, it must have been my opportunity for healing. I got everything I needed in that single visit to keep me going until she died. From the depths of my soul, sobbing uncontrollably, I said what I just didn't know how to say before then, but in that moment, the words flowed effortlessly as I said:

"All I ever wanted was for you to be proud of me, Mom. I love you so much, and because you saved my life, you gave me a gift I can never repay, and all I ever wanted for you in return was to be proud of me. For what you gave me all of those years, there is no way I'm going to leave you here and let you go through this alone. Besides, I know this is what Dad and Robbie would have wanted me to do."

Suddenly, what her mouth could not say, her eyes conveyed. I couldn't believe it. A single tear came streaming down her cheek with that signature smirk of hers. It was a cold, snowy Tuesday on February 19 when the woman I always knew as my childhood mother, Mrs. Doris Maxine Stanley Jenkins, died without ever saying good-bye.

Chapter 16
FORGIVENESS AND HOPE

Pick Yourself Up
Dust Yourself Off
Start All Over Again
—Frank Sinatra

What Is Forgiveness?

Can you abandon the justification to resent the people who unjustly hurt you? Can you provide compassion, demonstrate generosity, and even foster goodwill towards them? To do so from my experience is to forgive. So why bother to forgive? I don't know where or how I developed the capacity to forgive as a young child, but somehow I realized that forgiving the people who hurt me does not change the past, but it brightens the future

While there may be complex perspectives to consider under many circumstances, I found the following words helped me with the question "Why forgive?"

While I no longer practice Catholicism, as a little boy, while living with Mom and Dad Jenkins, biblical verses were instilled in me during religion classes at St. Francis of Assisi Catholic School. Taken from the New International Version of the Bible, Luke 6: 27-30 says:

27 "But I say to you who listen: Love your enemies, do good to those who hate you, 28 bless those who curse you, pray for those who mistreat you. 29 If anyone hits you on the cheek, offer the other also. And if anyone takes away your coat, don't hold back your shirt either. 30 Give to everyone who asks from you, and from one, who takes away your things, don't ask for them back. Another popular verse I learned that was equally impactful is "Forgive, and you will be forgiven" (Luke

6:37 NIV) Others such as the author Philip Yancey suggest that "To forgive is to set a prisoner free and discover that the prisoner was you," and author Marianne Williamson in *A Return to Love*; says" the practice of forgiveness is our most important contribution to the healing of the world," and recently, Pope Benedict XVI profoundly stated "Evil can be overcome only with forgiveness,"

The Qur'an describes the believers (Muslims) as those who "avoid gross sins and vice, and when angered, they forgive (Qur'an 42:37).

In Judaism, if a person causes harm, but then sincerely and honestly apologizes to the wronged individual and tries to rectify the wrong, the wronged individual is religiously required to grant forgiveness:

It is forbidden to be obdurate and not allow yourself to be appeased. On the contrary, one should be easily pacified and find it difficult to become angry. When asked by an offender for forgiveness, one should forgive with a sincere mind and a willing spirit ... forgiveness is natural to the seed of Israel. (Mishneh Torah, *Teshuvah* 2:10)

In Judaism, one must go to those he has harmed in order to be entitled to forgiveness. [One who sincerely apologizes three times for a wrong committed against another has fulfilled his or her obligation to seek forgiveness. (Shulchan Aruch) OC 606:1]

Addressing Dhritarashtra, Vidura said:

There is one only defect in forgiving persons, and not another; that defect is that people take a forgiving person to be weak. That defect, however, should not be taken into consideration, for forgiveness is a great power. Forgiveness is a virtue of the weak, and an ornament of the strong. Forgiveness subdues [all] in this world; what is there that forgiveness cannot achieve? What can a wicked person do unto him who carries the sabre of forgiveness in his hand? Fire falling on the grassless ground is extinguished of itself. And unforgiving individual defiles himself with many enormities. Righteousness is the one highest good; and forgiveness is the one supreme peace; knowledge is one supreme contentment; and benevolence, one sole happiness. (From the Mahabharata, Udyoga Parva Section XXXIII, translated by Sri Kisari Mohan Ganguli).

Christianity teaches through the Bible, "And when you stand praying, if you hold anything against anyone, forgive him, so that your Father in heaven may forgive you your sins" (Mark 11:25, New International Version); "But I tell you who hear me: Love your enemies, do good to those who hate you, bless those who curse you, pray for those who mistreat you. If someone strikes you on one cheek, turn to him the other also" (Luke 6:27–29, NIV); "Be merciful, just as your Father is merciful" (Luke 6:36, NIV); and "Do not judge, and you will not be judged. Do not condemn, and you will not be condemned.

I continue to struggle and "the hardest thing I had to learn in life was which bridge to cross and which to burn," as suggested by David L. Russell, but it was President John F. Kennedy who said that which appears to be the general case for most of us, albeit unconsciously or not—"Forgive your enemies, but never forget their names."

It is only because I believe that to forgive is to foster hope and to foster hope is to become free from the real prison where you are both the inmate and the jailer that I know it is not easy for us to do. Perhaps Mahatma Gandhi reminds us through his teachings that "The weak can never forgive. Forgiveness is the attribute of the strong." Perhaps this has become such a core value since childhood, because I know how much forgiveness I need.

My Journey to Forgiveness

I never thought that any of the people who abandoned or rejected me should ask me for forgiveness. Regardless of what they did, I needed to forgive them in order to believe and hope in the possibility of a better future. You see, my determination to survive the pain and grow from it was paramount. First, however, I had to free myself with the gift of forgiveness—a gift that, after all that I'd been through, I rightly deserved to take from my perpetrators. Only then could I let go of the anger and disappointment that was the prison of my pain. I understand that many have their opinions about whether or not child abusers are entitled to forgiveness. But with time and therapy, I was able to forgive and had to so that I could try to engage in healthy relationships going forward.

When I forgave my abusers, I also understood that the abuse was wrong and wanted nothing to do with most of them ever again. Where the pain is too deep, I don't have any desire to reconcile. Some have the misconception that forgiveness means you have to reconcile with people who have done you wrong or mistreated you, and that simply is not the case. The pain won't go away until you forgive, and I choose not to live in pain.

However, I don't want to mislead you and suggest that forgiveness is quick and easy. It is something that takes time when it is real and genuine. It took a good while for my grandmother and me to make peace with our past, but when we did, we were able to participate in the Present and enjoy a healthy relationship. Although I forgave Ma Jenkins, I regret that we never reconciled and got the chance to participate fully in a healthy relationship before she died. I'm certain she carried the hurt of our past to her grave, and for that, I am sad.

I relive those kinds of things from time to time, and I always have to forgive again and again, because sometimes I feel the pain all over again. However, as time goes on, the memories are not as strong, and I cope a lot better. I don't want my pain to block my peace. Instead, I want to be liberated. It is the peace within that I seek and that same peace can only be mine if I am willing to let go and cling to the hope that I can live my dream.

What Forgiveness Is Not

Remember when, as a child, you were forced by some adult to "forgive" someone who was first forced to "say sorry" to you? Is this really repentance by the perpetrator or forgiveness by the victim? Well, perhaps so—in a few rare cases. But let us be honest and acknowledge that this charade by children is more often a temporary cessation of hostilities for the sake of the grown-ups, with the full intent to do more of the same (and not get caught) and/or get revenge later, when beyond the adult's watchful eye. Adults will often engage children in this ritual, because strife in a family or group of kids is a rejected source of tension, and they want to teach. Play-acting does give at least a temporary reprieve. This childish pantomime of "forgiveness" often carries into adulthood as a superficial substitute for the real thing. We think by saying so, it is so.

Forgiveness is mistaken for many other things. Forgiveness is not:
- denial or minimization of the offense;
  - "It wasn't that bad, really."
  - "My sister had it so much worse than I did; I shouldn't even complain."
  - "You're overreacting."

- tolerating or condoning the offense;
  - "Sometimes, these things happen."
  - "Everybody makes mistakes."
  - "He was drunk, at the time."
- denial of the harmful effects;
  - "What doesn't kill you makes you stronger."
- justifying the offender's behavior;
  - "Maybe I deserved to be punished like that."
  - "If I hadn't done x, he wouldn't have done y."
- excusing the offender as if there is no blameworthiness or accountability;
  - "She couldn't help what she did."
  - "It's your fault for not stopping him or for not telling someone about it."
  - "Your daddy had a rough life himself as a child."
- canceling the consequences;
  - "He was really apologetic this time, so I want to drop the charges."
  - "If Mommy apologizes, and I forgive her, will the judge let me go back home?"
- owed to the offender;
  - "He apologized. Why must you hold a grudge?"
  - "It's wrong of you to hold this over her head forever."
- forgetting the offense;
  - "It's water under the bridge."
  - "Don't cry over spilled milk."
- remaining vulnerable to being hurt again;
  - "She learned her lesson and won't bother you again."
  - "You need to turn the other cheek."
- reverting to the relationship's original status;
  - "If you forgave me, why don't you trust me like you used to?"
- a decision by itself, rather than an involved process over time; or
  - "Last month, you told me you had decided to forgive them, but you obviously haven't."
- a quick fix or an easy escape from one's hurts.
  - "If you could just let go of your anger, you'd be a lot happier."

o   "The sooner you put it behind you, the better off you'll be."

"You will know that forgiveness has begun when you recall those who hurt you and feel the power to wish them well."
— Lewis B. Smedes, *Forgive and Forget:*
Healing the Hurts We Don't Deserve

When Children Have Been Mistreated

Trying to be "therapeutic" with children promotes the tendency to draw out the hard feelings (e.g., anger, hostility) about the past to be sure that they aren't suppressed. However, because children want to please parents, therapists, social workers, foster parents, and other adults, if they hear the message that we are only interested in their anger and resentment toward birth parents, they may tell us only what they think we want to hear. As a result, they may miss out on acknowledging the ambivalence they feel, which is part of the groundwork of forgiveness, whether they approach it now or later.

Allowing children this ambivalence, or helping them to acknowledge it, requires wisdom and sensitivity. Often, problems with healing and moving on come from situations in which the child has little or no ambivalence about the birth parents; either they are totally angry and blaming, or else they are numb, suppressing their anger and pain too much. They may need help to be in touch with all of their conflicting feelings. Ambivalence is healthy and expected for what they've been through.

It's important to take the high road and emphasize that the child doesn't need to turn against the birth family to show loyalty to the new family. For example, when a child expresses only hostility toward a birth parent, you might let them vent and then say "I really understand where you are with those feelings right now." Then over time, help them balance that position by reminding them that, for example, their mother gave them life or by asking, "Are there some things your parents did that showed they loved you or that you miss about them?" Foster parents can use examples from their own extended families to discuss and model acknowledging the good as well as the bad in others.

Seven Tips to Foster Forgiveness in Children Who Have Been Mistreated

1. Help them process feelings of shame and guilt. Start by strengthening secure attachment, trust, self-esteem, empathy, behavioral and emotional self-control, and healthy boundaries.

2. Make it clear to children that it is okay to have positive feelings about their birth parents and relatives and to grieve over losing their family connections. Often adults will give children mixed signals about this, even unintentionally. No matter how bad the situation in the birth family was, respect the biological bond.

3. Remain aware of the values, expectations, and general emotional baggage you bring to working with children around family relationships, painful experiences, and forgiveness. Don't project this on the children. Don't judge the feelings they express.

4. Try to help them open up. Without projecting an expectation that a child should forgive, be open to discussing any part of their past history that interests them, help them process all the feelings they have, and support them to the extent that they are ready to forgive. Children want and need to talk about what they've been through and are going through.

5. When a child is intent on engaging in forgiveness work, use questions to surface unrealistic expectations and "magical thoughts." The child may think that forgiving means making the pain go away or being able to rejoin the birth family. Ask, "What do you think forgiveness means?"; "What will it feel like when you have forgiven?"; "What do you think will happen if you forgive [the perpetrator]?" Avoid asking a child or youth to try to understand why a perpetrator hurt him or why others failed to protect him; children can confuse empathy with justification, and this can undermine other healing processes.

6. Though most children are not capable of deep forgiveness and despite the risk of premature forgiveness, some may actually accomplish genuine forgiveness. Advise the child

that the task of forgiving those who hurt them is likely to surface again as they grow up—in relationships, in times of loneliness or struggle, and when they have children of their own. Whether a child's forgiveness work is successful, unsuccessful, or incomplete at a given time, it is normal for everyone to rework painful issues at different life stages.

7. Children removed from their homes should have opportunities for continuing contact with birth families, within the limits of what is safe and healthy. Subsequently, as adults, they will have the option of reengaging with their birth families as part of healing. If contact with close family members is not possible or advisable, explore whether members of the extended family or family friends can be engaged with to continue a meaningful connection.

Hope: Picking Yourself Up

In his inauguration speech, President Barack Obama said, "Starting today, we must pick ourselves up, dust ourselves off, and begin again the work of remaking America." It echoed the lyrics from "Pick Yourself Up". Like the eloquence of our new president, those are lyrics both lofty and folksy; the song speaks of what we aspire to, what we hope to attain, but does so in the common language of the people.

Determined to rise above hopelessness on my journey, I discovered that, if you want change, you have to begin by *hoping* for change. Hope is the energy we need to rise beyond our pain, realize our dreams and achieve our desires.

How Do We Foster Hope?

Though becoming more hopeful is easier said than done, through overcoming adversities and working with youth challenged by the same things I have been through, I experienced the ability to raise dim hopes in the following ways:

- Building dreams with goals energizes hope. A goal is a purpose, motive, or reason for the use of time or for the justification of an activity. When we develop the capacity to dream, we begin the process that fosters hope. Our dreams enable us to create and examine the goals that emerge from our desires and ambitions. The likelihood of sustaining hope is greater the more these goals are:

- solid,
- possible,
- exciting, and
- challenging,
- Forgiving and accepting losses sustains hope. When we change something in our lives, there will be a loss of something we value. This could include the loss of relationships that are important, of an opportunity, of plans, or of a dream. Loss often leads to sadness and anger. Our willingness to talk honestly about the loss and to own these feelings represents the initial steps in mourning the loss. By grieving and forgiving, we acknowledge the loss, pain, or anger as something significant. We can then open ourselves to learning something from the experience and how to get on with our lives.
- Accepting and creating yourself is the path to hope. Knowledge of the skills and strengths we bring to the table generate hope.
- Leveraging healthy relationships fosters hope. Helpful people, resources, and friends—to get their perspectives and support—are good ways to reconcile your dreams with strategies that optimize your success.

Every child has potential, and every life has value. Sadly, many of us with deep-rooted pain from experiences of neglect, abandonment, or abuse are robbed of our ability to enjoy life, experience our potentials, and discover the purpose for existing on earth.

When a child is connected to a caring adult, they can facilitate experiences through relationships that begin the journey of forgiveness and the acceptance of losses. The capacity to dream of a brighter future rooted in goals that are achievable can begin as hope is fostered. Let's be ever mindful that, individually and collectively, we all benefit from contributing to ensuring that children are connected and valued. Fostering hope for one another enables us to escape the prisons of pain to enjoy purposeful lives in communities that are safe and vibrant.

Along with my faith in God, though my troubles may come from time to time, they do not last forever. Because of this life lesson, I developed seven affirmations that help me show up each day, prepared to live the dream with my name on it.

Affirmations Fostering My Hope

1. I will show up today, equipped to participate fully in relationships by forgiving those who hurt me and by seeking forgiveness from those I hurt.
2. I will show up today, believing in the dream with my name on it, and chase it down.
3. I will show up today, giving no one the power to kill my dreams or break my spirit.
4. I will show up today, with the passion to change the things I can and the courage to accept those things I cannot.
5. I will show up today confident that every experience will teach, strengthen, and prepare me for my destiny.
6. I will show up today, with determination to find something beautiful or create something beautiful.
7. I believe each day is a new beginning, and I am prepared to learn, to do my best, and to overcome.

The challenges we face in life can be burdensome. However, we must find the dreams with our names on them, believe in them, and then hold on, determined to make those dreams come true. Besides the belief in ourselves and the dreams, the capacity to function in healthy relationships is critical to living our dreams. When bad experiences with people fracture the human spirit, the capacity to overcome is fueled, when possible, by forgiveness or letting go of the past and by hope in clinging to the future. It is through connections and bonds that we establish with other caring people that our dreams are encouraged and reinforced. This is the primary reason I sought, with the support of the National CASA Association and many others, to develop CASA for Children of DC with the goal of engaging individuals, corporations, and communities to restore hope in children and families shattered through tragic life experiences.

While living in Rego Park group home at sixteen years old, I was given a card with the words of Nobel Peace Prize recipient and Civil Rights leader, Dr. Martin Luther King. This quotation on the card sits eye view and framed in my office. "The true neighbor will risk his position, his prestige, and even his life for the welfare of others. Even through dangerous valleys and hazardous pathways, he will lift some bruised and beaten brother to a higher and more noble life. This is the greatest influence that fuels my determination to leverage my life for the uplifting of those behind traveling the journey through abuse, abandonment and repeated rejection.

The consequences to society for each of us ignoring each other's pain, particularly children who've been abused or neglected, are incalculable. You don't have to go far to find communities of angry children retaliating without regard to or dreams for the future, because we are not responding to their basic needs.

It is my wish that something from my journey might help you to find the dream with your name on it while embracing the truth that makes all of us interdependent. As we commit to overcoming the pain of our past, which maybe preventing us from participating in the present, we can discover our collective purpose and help cultivate the dreams of our youth and their belief in the possibilities that foster the hope required to make them come true.

We must value and nurture every child's potential. Sadly, many of our children have so much deep-rooted pain that it has become a prison that locks up their potential. When they are consumed with rejection and pain, it prevents them from dreaming and hoping. Without hope, there's despair and trouble. But it doesn't have to be that way; we can each restore hope, one child at a time.

There is one particular area where Americans can enact great change. Stark statistics highlight a specific, societal need.

Foster Care in the Year 2020, from CASEY Family Programs (if nothing changes in child welfare trends from 2005 to 2020)

- Children who will experience the foster care system: 10,500,000
- Children who will age out of the foster care system: 300,000
- Foster youth who age out of the system who will experience homelessness: 75,000
- Foster youth who age out of the system who will graduate from college: 9,000
- Number of children who will be killed by abuse or neglect: 22,500

Chapter 17
SOMEBODY TOLD ME

Somebody told me to deliver this message...
See the child who's dying of hunger and another man who's doing good?
He's wondering why that man's not even wondering
how to help that baby if he could
—Teddy Pendergrass

As we participate in our own journey of discovery—whether as a relative, friend, or volunteer—we can each commit to finding our own ways of restoring hope to a child or to a struggling adult in need. I share my journey, which is rooted in pain, forgiveness, and hope, with gratitude to all who helped me; although winds may arise and storms may blow, hope endures as you find, believe, and live the dream with your name on it.

Unfortunately, child abuse continues to be a national problem and poses many challenges for our communities, the child welfare system, and the medical and legal structures. It's not someone else's problem; it's everybody's problem.

We have to rethink the foster care system in general. Beyond the effects of neglect and abuse, foster children are children first, children like the ones in our own families, who need a kind word, a loving gesture, and a helping hand. Do you realize your capacity to foster hope? Your capacity to impact lives? You may, through a simple deed, help someone develop the capacity to not only dream again but begin believing that his or her dreams can come true. .

I believe that, more now than ever, we must invest greater resources to support and keep families together. My experience is not mine alone. Once youth enter the foster care system, they are likely to be further traumatized as circumstances force movement from home to home. Pilot programs in Washington DC and other cities across the nation demonstrate the possibilities for our children and youth, created of our collective will. To break the cycle of abuse and neglect, we must establish easily accessible, comprehensive, community-based resources that support the family unit, extended family members, and neighbors; are culturally sensitive and competent; and address both the strengthening of parenting skills and basic health issues.

If children must enter the system, we can all consider training to become a culturally competent CASA (Court Appointed Special Advocate) to ensure that not one slips between the cracks. Perhaps a culturally competent CASA from the South Bronx or a surrounding area would have identified resources for the treatment my mother needed, and if she had chosen not to accept that support, would have expedited the process of terminating her parental rights. Granted, things were different then, but it would have been an enormous help to have had another set of eyes capable of keeping track of all the players in the system and that could have supplied child specific information to the system's judges.

Over the years, I've seen increasing numbers of youth welfare decisions and policies revictimize children and perpetuate their troubles. We must engage people as partners in their own destinies and recognize that governments make bad parents when they try to do it without engaging the community as part of the solution. I've seen a greater leveraging of the perspectives from youth who are aging through systems. This was unimaginable when I entered the national landscape with my first speech "No Place to Go Back To" over twenty years ago.

Although this change is certainly encouraging, the transition of leaving foster care at ages eighteen or twenty-one is still ineffectively addressed. Most kids who age out of the system are completely unprepared for the challenges they will face on their own. Services to support them either do not exist or are not coordinated properly.

The system's revolving door leaves most of its "graduates" more abused and neglected than they had been before arriving, with limited capacity to engage in healthy relationships, with few job skills, and with no one to turn to for support.

Did you know that research indicates that 33 percent of homeless people and 80 percent of our prison population were once in foster care? The numbers are equally alarming when it comes to those in mental health institutions. Far too many children can't beat those depressing odds on their own, but the presence of caring adults could provide the hope necessary to get them over life's hurdles.

The tragedy is that there is no yardstick that the public can use to measure the relative success or failure of those entrusted with raising victimized children. It's astonishing to think that we apply higher accountability standards to our car mechanics than we do to child welfare administrators. I don't think anyone would keep sending a new BMW or Land Rover to the same auto shop if it came back inoperable or more damaged than when it had been taken in for service.

Why, then, would any reasonable, taxpaying citizen tolerate a system in which the children removed from families where abuse or neglect occurred are further traumatized in foster care through multiple moves or, even worse, are revictimized through sexual, emotional, and physical abuse?

Because child welfare agencies do such a poor job of preparing youth for adulthood, I think that foster care children should be guaranteed lifelong benefits comparable to those provided (and rightly so) to our military veterans. They too are veterans, but of a different kind of war. The act of removing a child from his or her home implies a permanent commitment on the part of the government to that child's welfare. How does anyone in good conscience dare to remove children from their families without ensuring that the caretakers can provide those children with a brighter future that maximizes their potentials?

According to a study released by Casey Family Programs and Harvard Medical School, adults who were formerly in foster care have up to twice the rate of post-traumatic stress disorder (PTSD) as United States war veterans. Although opinions differ regarding entitlement programs, not only is providing services for our foster care graduates morally right, but investing in such services is economically sound when compared to the cost of long-term institutionalization in mental health facilities or prisons—the end of the line for many of the victims of a failed system.

While radical I must admit, I call upon our policy makers to pass legislation that gives children raised in foster care the following safety net, at the very least, comparable to that they would have if raised in a middle-class family. Like veterans of war, I believe we should provide variations of the following to youth raised and parented by the government.

1. Lifetime access to Veterans Administration Hospitals for mental health services. Many of the mental health problems found in foster children (such as PTSD, depression, and drug addiction) are also seen in soldiers returning from combat, the military or veterans' health care facilities could be used to treat mental health issues that can emerge at any time in the lives of victims of neglect or child abuse (Pecora et al, 2005).

2. Lifetime access to educational benefits that cap at a reasonable dollar amount. This plan will enable former foster care children to complete their educations when they are mentally and emotionally mature, instead of mandating that eighteen-year-olds immediately leave the system with the expectation that they are equipped and disciplined to further their education based solely on their chronological age.

3. Comparable home ownership benefits to what veterans receive.

4. Supportive housing, similar to halfway houses, during times of crisis that result from unstable living conditions, poor mental health, limited education, or underemployment. Most of us can rely on our families as a safe haven throughout our lives and to provide support during difficult times. Most foster care veterans don't have that option.

5. Greater accountability of guardians and mental health providers to ensure that they promote relationship building, conflict resolution, and problem-solving skills while children are in foster care. When things become difficult in a foster family, the family often abandons the child and/or allows the child to abandon the relationship instead of working the problem through. These disruptions mean that abused or neglected children rarely learn how to participate in healthy relationships. Caregivers must help

abused and neglected children work through the issues that this kind of trauma creates. If children of abuse and neglect are encouraged to live in the present and to develop the tools that provide healing from their pain, then they will have a better chance to discover the purpose of their lives and to find the motivation to make their dreams come true.

But legislation is not enough. Our religious leaders, congregations, sororities, fraternities, and all civic-minded groups must embrace and provide basic support for youths who are transitioning from foster care back to their communities. A safe place to stay during semester breaks, letters of encouragement, or care packages while attending college, are just a few examples of how we can provide encouragement. Thus, we contribute to breaking cycles of abandonment, abuse, and neglect and restoring hope.

It is critical that those who work with a child identified as a "youth at risk" must first believe and hope in all that is possible and then live in that truth. To do that, we must visualize, with enthusiasm, a bright future for that child—just as most birth parents dream for their own children. I have met many caregivers throughout the country whose actions and words reflect the belief that a child's current reality determines his fate. I reject the notion that there ever existed a social condition of doom and gloom. My survival and that of countless others enabled me to stand witness that this predestination theory is not fact.

If the best you can do is ignore those in need around you or declare that "you already know where he'll end up," then consider yourself a contributor to the circumstances and belief systems that cause him to end up there. But if you can just take an interest in your neighbor's child with an occasional visit, call, or simply a kind word, consider yourself a facilitator of dreams that foster hope.

I'm reminded of when I interviewed for a position at a renowned medical institution located in Baltimore, Maryland, that provides therapeutic foster care and a host of comprehensive services for special needs children. After completing my interviews with a licensed clinical social worker, a psychiatrist, and three other members of the executive management team, I withdrew my name from consideration as a finalist, because, once they learned I had been a foster child, they all focused (with different variations) on wanting to know what made me so extraordinary and why I had made it. While there is nothing fundamentally wrong with that question, it became clear that they didn't believe my professional accomplishments were something the children they served in foster care were really capable of achieving. Why bother if you don't believe in your capacity to restore hope?

Children today still need what I needed when I was a child: the support of caring, committed adults who believe in their possibilities. I also needed well-qualified professionals to help me resolve conflicts and build attachments so that I could engage in nurturing, long-term relationships in the future, instead of constantly running from or sabotaging good connections. We should be as concerned about ensuring that youth have the psychological, social, and emotional skills necessary for healthy adult living as we are about whether they have an apartment upon emancipation. Without such skills, when the going gets tough, the apartment will be abandoned, and running instead of seeking support to resolve problems is the most familiar coping strategy. As the old folks use to say, let me make it plain: if you think they *won't* make it, they'll feel your vibe and probably won't. If you believe they *can* make it, they'll feel your vibe and probably will. If you *teach* and show them how to make it, they'll develop the confidence to make it, and yours will be a job well done.

I hope you see that mine has been an incredible journey through trouble and triumph. The true blessing is that, although I have been scorned and covered with scars, I am still strong, determined, and full of courage. My determination to make it to the finish line is fueled by seeing the effect that a terrible multigenerational legacy of drugs, neglect, and abuse has had on my family. Moreover, discover my potential to achieve and rise above that troubled legacy, emulated from the ability to forgive and seek forgiveness. As you put this book down, think of someone who needs to hear a reminder from you that we are not our mistakes; we are our possibilities.

With the hope we have within, let's help some bruised or beaten brother and find the dreams with their names on them. Perhaps it begins with your personal determination to find healing from the pain that imprisons you from achieving your dreams and becoming your best self. I know my grandmother is happy that I'm sharing our lesson with you.

This all seems so unbelievable to me. It's like I'm living somebody else's life. What a blessing for me to experience in one lifetime. This man called Shane, once a desperate child in search of the love and the security that a family brings, became a teenage, single parent and is parenting children through birth and adoption. Life does come full circle and hope endures. Now, as the founder of CASA for Children of DC, an organization that trains volunteers to advocate for abused and neglected children, my multitude of humbling experiences continue to build on itself. If I can simply leverage my experience to bring attention to the threats compromising the healthy development of children while developing strategies that will strengthen families, then my life wasn't in vain.

Never did I desire to become an author, but I was born with this book inside of me. How could I have ever imagined as a little boy that I'd become the founder and leader of a grassroots movement on behalf of children who are hurting in the way I did. However, as a man, I've found that it's important to be reminded from time to time that our journey is shared by others and that peace, success, and happiness are within our grasp. We can each become a true neighbor, willing, in the words of Martin Luther King Jr., "to risk [your] position, prestige, and even life for the welfare of others. In dangerous valleys and hazardous pathways, [you] could strive to lift some bruised and beaten brother to a higher and nobler life." It takes so little to be a resource and foster hope for a friend, child, or shattered family. If you can't adopt, be a foster parent. If you can't be a foster parent, be a CASA volunteer or help out at a neighborhood center. What you get back will be far greater than everything you gave. We are each a critical part of the solution.

The national movement to make sure that victims of child abuse or neglect are heard in court began in the 1960s. Judges realized that they were making far-reaching decisions about the lives of children without hearing the unique perspectives of those children. Some judges asked social workers or friends to informally investigate child abuse cases and to make recommendations about what would best serve the needs and interests of the children involved.

The first volunteer guardian *ad litem* (GAL) program serving abused and neglected children was organized by King County Judge David Soukup in 1977 in Seattle, Washington. Word of the success of the King County program spread like wildfire, and similar programs began all over the United States. Because some state statutes require the GAL to be an attorney, the term court-appointed special advocate (CASA) was coined to describe volunteers from the local community who are trained to serve as advocates for abused and neglected children involved in juvenile court proceedings.

In 1982, the National CASA Association, Inc., was established to serve as an umbrella organization for the growing number of programs in the country. The National CASA Association provides information, technical assistance, research, and training; sponsors an annual national conference; and has a grants program that annually awards millions of dollars to state and local CASA and GAL programs. Membership in the National CASA Association is open to both individuals and programs.

At CASA for Children of the District of Columbia, just like at CASA programs all across the United States, we recruit, train, and supervise community volunteers who serve as court-appointed special advocates. Those advocates must meet national standards, and they investigate, recommend to judges, and monitor legal actions that are in the best interests of individual children who are victims of child abuse and neglect.

The goal of CASA is to see that each child is placed as quickly as possible in a permanent home that is safe, nurturing, and free of violence. In a system where dockets overflow and professional caseloads make individual attention challenging, volunteers ensure that the needs of each child are met. By providing objective, detailed information and recommendations to the courts, volunteers help to move the children through the child welfare system and into adoptive families as quickly as possible.

Volunteers, dedicated staff members, and a committed board of directors work together at this nonprofit youth advocacy agency. CASA volunteers are an ethnically and culturally diverse group. They receive thirty hours of training with experts in the field, and each volunteer is carefully evaluated before being assigned to a case.

CASA emphasizes collaboration to ensure that each child will be able to return home or find a new adoptive family. We know that courtroom advocacy alone, even with hundreds of committed volunteers, will not produce good outcomes. Only widespread community support will enable us to meet the multiple needs of our children, especially for kinship, foster, and adoptive homes.

You can get on board and become a part of this movement, which is led by the people for the people. We need more CASA volunteers of color from the communities where the greatest numbers of children enter foster care. We need ordinary citizens who are willing to step up and get to know children, to make sure that those children are never overlooked or forgotten, and to hold their government and themselves responsible for ensuring that children who are abused and neglected have a chance to achieve their full potentials and be nurtured as they transition into adulthood. CASA volunteers go into court with the children and help judges make the best possible decision about where the children should live, what schools the children should attend, and what educational resources the children need. They are the children's voices in court.

You can perform those crucial services after just thirty hours of training. Our children need us now. So do not let another day go by. Put this book down, and call 1-800-628-3223 or visit www.nationalcasa.org to find the CASA program near you. Low CASA caseloads allow volunteers to obtain complete information about each child, which means that the courts can make better decisions about each child's welfare. CASA volunteers handle just one or two cases at a time and give each child the sustained personal attention that he or she deserves.

Complex cases with multiple risk factors receive more attention so they can move forward in a timely manner. You can help foster hope for children in DC now. Please consider making a generous, tax-deductible contribution to:

CASA for Children of DC
Attention: Fostering Hope
515 M Street, SE
Washington, DC 20003

Appendixes

Appendix A: The National Scope of Child Abuse

Each week, child protective service (CPS) agencies throughout the United States receive more than 50,000 reports of suspected child abuse or neglect. In approximately two-thirds of these cases, the information in the report was sufficient to prompt an assessment or investigation. Approximately 896,000 children have been found to have been victims of abuse or neglect, an average of more than 2,450 children per day.

Approximately four children die every day because of child abuse or neglect. More than half (60 percent) of those 2,450 victims experienced neglect, meaning a caretaker failed to provide for their basic needs. Nearly 20 percent were physically abused, and 10 percent were sexually abused; these cases are typically the ones that are publicized. The smallest numbers (7 percent) were victims of emotional abuse, which includes a caretaker criticizing, rejecting, or refusing to nurture a child.

No group of children is immune. Boys and girls are about equally likely to be abused or neglected, and the phenomenon occurs in all races and ethnicities. On average, 54 percent of all victims are Caucasian, 26 percent are African-American, and 11 percent are Hispanic. American Indian or Alaska Native children accounted for 2 percent of victims, and 1 percent were Asian Pacific Islanders. Children of all ages experience abuse and neglect, but the youngest children are most vulnerable. Children younger than one-year-old account for about 41 percent of all abuse-related deaths, and 76 percent of those killed are younger than four.

Of all reports made to CPS agencies, 57 percent came from professionals who came in contact with the abused child (16 percent from teachers; 16 percent from legal, law enforcement, and criminal justice personnel; 13 percent from social service workers; and 8 percent from medical personnel). Many people in those professions are required by law to report suspected abuse or neglect. The other 43 percent of the reports came from nonprofessional sources (such as parents, other relatives, friends, and neighbors), 10 percent of which reports were anonymous.

It is important for everyone to know the signs that may indicate maltreatment and how to report it. We all have a responsibility to keep children safe as we take steps to prevent abuse from occurring in the first place. For more information about recognizing child abuse and neglect, see *Recognizing Child Abuse and Neglect: Signs and Symptoms* on the National Clearinghouse on Child Abuse and Neglect Information Web site (http://nccanch.acf.hhs.gov/pubs/factsheets/signs.cfm.).

Appendix B: Statistics on Children and Youth in Care

(All data are for the period ending September 30, 2001, and are taken from the Casey Family Program's "Child Welfare Fact Sheet" dated March 15, 2004.)

- 542,000 children and youth are in foster care on any given day in the United States.
- Nearly half of all children in foster care are over the age of ten.
- African-American children and children of two or more races are four times more likely than Caucasian children to be placed in out-of-home care (CASEY Family Programs, 2000).
- Children of color are less likely to be reunified with their birth families (Hill, 2001).
- Children of color experience a higher number of placements.
- American Indian and Alaska Native children are three times more likely than Caucasian children to be placed in out-of-home care.
- Approximately 100,000 youths in foster care are sixteen or older.
- Approximately 20,000 youths aged sixteen and older make the transition from foster care to legal emancipation each year.

Appendix C: Consequences of Child Abuse and Neglect

Factors Affecting the Consequences of Child Abuse

The impact of child abuse and neglect is often discussed in terms of physical, psychological, behavioral, and societal consequences. In reality, however, it is impossible to separate those consequences completely. Physical consequences (such as damage to a child's growing brain) can have psychological implications (cognitive delays or emotional difficulties, for example). Psychological problems often manifest as high-risk behaviors. Depression and anxiety, for example, may make a person more likely to smoke, abuse alcohol or illicit drugs, or overeat. High-risk behaviors, in turn, can lead to long-term physical health problems such as sexually transmitted diseases, cancer, and obesity.

This fact sheet provides an overview of some of the most common physical, psychological, behavioral, and societal consequences of child abuse and neglect, while acknowledging that much crossover among categories exists.

Physical Health Consequences

Not all abused and neglected children will experience long-term consequences. Outcomes of individual cases vary widely and are affected by a combination of factors, including:

- the child's age and developmental status when the abuse or neglect occurred;the type of abuse (physical abuse, neglect, sexual abuse, etc.);
- the frequency, duration, and severity of abuse; and
- the relationship between the victim and his or her abuser (Chalk, Gibbons, and Scarupa 2002).

Researchers have also begun to explore why, given similar conditions, some children experience long-term consequences of abuse and neglect while others emerge relatively unscathed. The ability to cope, and even thrive, following a negative experience is sometimes referred to as resilience. A number of protective factors may contribute to an abused or neglected child's resilience. These include individual characteristics, such as optimism, self-esteem, intelligence, creativity, humor, and independence. Protective factors can also include the family or social environment, such as a child's access to social support and, in particular, a caring adult in the child's life. Community well-being, including neighborhood stability and access to health care, is also a protective factor (Thomlison 1997).

The immediate physical effects of abuse or neglect can be relatively minor (bruises or cuts) or severe (broken bones, hemorrhage, or even death). In some cases, the physical effects are temporary; however, the pain and suffering they cause a child should not be discounted.

Meanwhile, the long-term impact of child abuse and neglect on physical health is just beginning to be explored. Below are some outcomes researchers have identified.

- Shaken Baby Syndrome: The immediate effects of shaking a baby (a common form of child abuse in infants) can include vomiting, concussion, respiratory distress, seizures, and death. Long-term consequences can include blindness, learning disabilities, mental retardation, cerebral palsy, or paralysis (Conway 1998).

- Impaired Brain Development: Child abuse and neglect have been shown, in some cases, to cause important regions of the brain to fail to form properly, resulting in impaired physical, mental, and emotional development (Perry 2002; Shore 1997). In other cases, the stress of chronic abuse causes a hyperarousal response by certain areas of the brain, which may result in hyperactivity, sleep disturbances, and anxiety, as well as increased vulnerability to post-traumatic stress disorder, attention deficit/hyperactivity disorder, conduct disorder, and learning and memory difficulties (Perry 2001; Dallam 2001).

- Poor Physical Health: A study of 700 children who had been in foster care for one year found that more than one quarter of the children had some kind of recurring physical or mental health problem (National Survey of Child and Adolescent Well-Being). A study of 9,500 HMO participants showed a relationship between various forms of household dysfunction (including childhood abuse) and long-term health problems such as sexually transmitted diseases, heart disease, cancer, chronic lung disease, skeletal fractures, and liver disease (Hillis, Anda, Felitti, Nordenberg, and Marchbanks 2000; Felitti, Anda,

Nordenberg, Williamson, Spitz, Edwards, Koss, and Marks 1998).

Psychological Consequences

The immediate emotional effects of abuse and neglect—isolation, fear, and an inability to trust—can translate into lifelong consequences, including low self-esteem, depression, and relationship difficulties. Researchers have identified links between child abuse and neglect and the following:

- Poor Mental and Emotional Health: In one long-term study, as many as 80 percent of young adults who had been abused met the diagnostic criteria for at least one psychiatric disorder at age twenty-one. These young adults exhibited many problems, including depression, anxiety, eating disorders, and suicide attempts (Silverman, Reinherz, and Giaconia 1996). Other psychological and emotional conditions associated with abuse and neglect includes panic disorder, dissociative disorders, attention-deficit/ hyperactivity disorder, post-traumatic stress disorder, and reactive attachment disorder (Teicher 2000).

- Cognitive Difficulties: The National Survey of Child and Adolescent Well-Being recently found that children placed in out-of-home care due to abuse or neglect tended to score lower than the general population on measures of cognitive capacity, language development, and academic achievement (2003).

- Social Difficulties: Children who are abused and neglected by caretakers often do not form secure attachments to them. These early attachment difficulties can lead to later difficulties in relationships with other adults as well as with peers (Morrison, Frank, Holland, and Kates 1999).

Behavioral Consequences

Not all victims of child abuse and neglect will experience behavioral consequences; however, child abuse and neglect appear to make the following more likely:

- Difficulties during Adolescence: Studies have found abused and neglected children to be at least 25 percent more likely to experience problems such as delinquency, teen pregnancy, low academic achievement, drug use, and mental health problems (Kelley et al. 1997).

- Juvenile Delinquency and Adult Criminality: A National Institute of Justice study indicated being abused or neglected as a child increased the likelihood of arrest as a juvenile by 59 percent. Abuse and neglect increased the likelihood of adult criminal behavior by 28 percent and violent crime by 30 percent (Widom and Maxfield 2001).

- Alcohol and Other Drug Abuse: Research consistently reflects an increased likelihood that abused and neglected children will smoke cigarettes, abuse alcohol, or take illicit drugs. According to the National Institute on Drug Abuse, as many as two-thirds of people in drug treatment programs reported being abused as children (2000).

- Abusive behavior: Abusive parents have often experienced abuse during their own childhoods. It is estimated that approximately one-third of abused and neglected children will eventually victimize their own children (Prevent Child Abuse New York 2001).

Societal Consequences

While child abuse and neglect almost always occur within the family, the impact does not end there. Society as a whole pays a price for child abuse and neglect in terms of both direct and indirect costs.

- Direct costs include those associated with maintaining a child welfare system to investigate allegations of child abuse and neglect, as well as expenditures by the judicial, law enforcement, health, and mental health systems to respond to and treat abused children and their families. A report by Prevent Child Abuse America estimates these costs at $24 billion per year.

- Indirect costs represent the long-term economic consequences of child abuse and neglect. These include juvenile and adult criminal activity, mental illness, substance abuse, and domestic violence. They can also include loss of productivity due to unemployment and underemployment, the cost of special education services, and increased use of the health care system. Prevent Child Abuse America recently estimated these costs at more than $69 billion per year (2001).

Much research has been done about the possible consequences of child abuse and neglect. The effects vary depending on the circumstances of the abuse or neglect, the personal characteristics of the child, and the child's environment. Consequences may be mild or severe; they may disappear after a short period or last a lifetime; and they affect the child physically, psychologically, behaviorally, or in some combination of all three ways. Ultimately, due to related costs to public entities such as the health care, human services, and educational systems, abuse and neglect impact not just the child and family, but society as a whole.

Appendix D: Adult Survivors' Resources

The following organizations are among many that have information on adult survivors of child abuse. They are provided for public use by the National Clearinghouse on Child Abuse and Neglect. If you are aware of any others, please contact them at the information listed below.

Inclusion on this list is for information purposes and does not constitute an endorsement by the Clearinghouse or the Children's Bureau.

American Psychological Association (APA)
750 First Street NE
Washington, DC 20002
Phone: (202) 336-5500
Toll-Free: (800) 374-2721
URL: http://www.apa.org/

The American Psychological Association is a national scientific and professional organization representing the field of psychology. The APA offers a wide range of programs and services including a consumer help center, media information, a research office, and a section on public interest topics such as disabilities, ethnic minorities, and issues involving children, youth, and families.

Child Abuse Prevention Network
E-mail: tom@child-abuse.com
URL: http://child-abuse.com/capn.shtml

The Child Abuse Prevention Network, originally launched as an outreach effort of the Family Life Development Center at Cornell University, is sponsored by LifeNET, Inc. Through the World Wide Web, the network provides professionals with online tools and support for the identification, investigation, treatment, adjudication, and prevention of child abuse and neglect.

Childhelp USA
15757 North 78th Street
Scottsdale, AZ 85260
Phone: (480) 922-8212
Fax: (480) 922-7061
TDD: (800) 2-A-CHILD
Toll-Free: (800) 4-A-CHILD
URL: http://www.childhelpusa.org

Childhelp USA is dedicated to meeting the physical, emotional, educational, and spiritual needs of abused and neglected children by focusing its efforts and resources in the areas of treatment, prevention, and research. Its programs and services include the operation of the Childhelp USA National Child Abuse Hotline, residential treatment facilities for severely abused children, child advocacy centers that reduce the trauma of child abuse victims during the interview and examination process, group homes, foster family selection, training and certification, Head Start programs for at-risk children, child abuse prevention programs, and community outreach.

Darkness to Light
247 Meeting Street
Charleston, SC 29401
Phone: (843) 965-5444
Fax: (843) 965-5449
Toll-Free: 1-866- FOR-
LIGHT
(1-866-367-5444)
URL: http://www.
darkness2light.org/

Darkness to Light is primarily a prevention
program whose mission is to engage adults in
the prevention of child sexual abuse; to reduce
the incidence of child sexual abuse nationally
through education and public awareness aimed
at adults; and to provide adults with information
to recognize and react responsibly to child sexual
abuse.

National Clearinghouse
on Child Abuse
and Neglect Information
330 C Street, SW
Washington, DC 20447
Phone: (703) 385-7565
Fax: (703) 385-3206
Toll-Free: (800) FYI-3366
E-mail: nccanch@caliber.
com
URL: http://nccanch.acf.
hhs.gov

The National Clearinghouse on Child Abuse and
Neglect Information, a service of the Children's
Bureau, helps professionals locate information
on child abuse and neglect and child welfare,
fact sheets, resource lists, bulletins, and other
publications. Jointly with the National Adoption
Information Clearinghouse (NAIC), the National
Clearinghouse on Child Abuse and Neglect
Information publishes the *Children's Bureau
Express*, an online digest of news and resources for
professionals concerned with child maltreatment,
child welfare, and adoption.

National Institute of
Mental Health (NIMH)
6001 Executive Boulevard
Room 8184, MSC 9663
Bethesda, MD 20892-
9663
Phone: (301) 443-4513
Fax: (301) 443-4279
URL: http://www.nimh.
nih.gov

The National Institute of Mental Health
works to diminish the burden of mental illness
through research. NIMH seeks to achieve
better understanding, treatment, and eventually
prevention of mental illness.

Office for Victims of Crime (OVC)
810 7th Street NW
Washington, DC 20531
Phone: (202) 307-5983
TTY: (877) 712-9279
Toll-Free: (800) 627-6872
E-mail: askovc@ojp.usdoj.gov
URL: http://www.ojp.usdoj.gov/ovc/

The Office for Victims of Crimes was established by the 1984 Victims of Crime Act (VOCA) to oversee diverse programs that benefit victims of crime. OVC provides substantial funding to state victim assistance and compensation programs, the lifeline services that help victims to heal. The agency also supports training designed to educate criminal justice and allied professionals on the rights and needs of crime victims. OVC is one of five bureaus and four offices with grant-making authority within the Office of Justice Programs of the United States Department of Justice.

Safer Society Foundation, Inc.
P.O. Box 340
Brandon, VT 05733-0340
Phone: (802) 247-3132
Fax: (802) 247-4233
URL: http://www.safersociety.org/

The Safer Society Foundation, Inc., a nonprofit agency, is a national research, advocacy, and referral center on the prevention and treatment of sexual abuse. The foundation provides training and consultation, research, sex offender treatment referrals, a computerized program network, and a resource library. It also publishes materials for the prevention and treatment of sexual abuse.

Sidran Institute
200 East Joppa Road
Suite 207
Towson, MD 21286
Phone: (410) 825-8888
Fax: (410) 337-0747
E-mail: sidran@sidran.org
URL: http://www.sidran.org/

The Sidran Institute, a leader in traumatic stress education and advocacy, is a nationally focused nonprofit organization devoted to helping people who have experienced traumatic life events. The institute promotes improved understanding of the early recognition and treatment of trauma-related stress in children, the long-term effects of trauma on adults, and strategies that lead to the greatest success in self-help recovery for trauma survivors. The Sidran Institute also advocates clinical practices considered successful in aiding trauma victims and the development of public policy initiatives that are responsive to the needs of adult and child survivors of traumatic events.

References

Abhayagiri Buddhist Monastery. Preparing for death. 2008. http://www.abhayagiri.org/index.php/main/article/preparing_for_death/#top. Retrieved June 19, 2006.Universal Loving Kindness. 2009. http://www.abhayagiri.org/index.php/main/article/universal_loving_kindness/#top. Retrieved February 7, 2009-02-07.CASEY Family Programs, Child Welfare Fact Sheet, (Washington DC: U.S. Government Printing Office, 2009). Available online at http://www.casey.org/.

Chalk, R., A. Gibbons, and H. J. Scarupa. *The Multiple Dimensions of Child Abuse and Neglect: New Insights into an Old Problem.* Washington, DC: Child Trends, 2002. Also available online: www.childtrends.org/files/ChildAbuseRB.pdf

Conway, E. E. 1998. Nonaccidental head injury in infants: The shaken baby syndrome revisited. *Pediatric Annals, 27(10),* 677–690.

Dallam, S. J. The long-term medical consequences of childhood maltreatment. In *The Cost of Child Maltreatment: Who Pays? We All Do*, eds. K. Franey, R. Geffner, and R. Falconer. San Diego: Family Violence & Sexual Assault Institute, 2001.

Felitti, V. J., R. F. Anda, D. Nordenberg, D. F. Williamson, A. M. Spitz, V. Edwards, M. P. Koss, and J. S. Marks. 1998. Relationship of childhood abuse and household dysfunction to many of the leading causes of death in adults: The adverse childhood experiences (ACE) study. *American Journal of Preventive Medicine 14(4),* 245–258.

Goldman, J., M. K. Salus, D. Wolcott, and K. Y. Kennedy *A Coordinated Response to Child Abuse and Neglect: The Foundation for Practice.* Child Abuse and Neglect User Manual Series. Washington, DC: Government Printing Office, 2003.

Hill, R. "The Role of Race in Parental Reunification." (Paper presented at the Race Matters Forum Meeting, 2001).

Hillis, S. D., R. F. Anda, V. J. Felitti, D. Nordenberg, and P. A. Marchbanks. 2000. Adverse childhood experiences and sexually transmitted diseases in men and women: A retrospective study. *Pediatrics, 106(1).*

JewFAQ discussion of forgiveness on Yom Kippur. 2008. http://www.jewsuc.org/holiday4.htm. Retrieved April 26, 2008.

Kaufman, L. (2005)

Kelley, B. T., T. P. Thornberry, and C. A. Smith. *In the Wake of Childhood Maltreatment.* Washington, DC: National Institute of Justice, 1997.

Morrison, J. A., S. J. Frank, C. C. Holland, and W. R. Kates. Emotional development and disorders in young children in the child welfare system. In *Young Children and Foster Care; A Guide for Professionals,* eds. J. A. Silver, B. J. Amster, and T. Haecker, 33–64. Baltimore, MD: Paul H. Brookes, 1999.

National Clearinghouse on Child Abuse and Neglect Information. 2001. In focus: Understanding the effects of maltreatment on early brain development. http://nccanch.acf.hhs.gov/pubs/focus/earlybrain.cfm. Accessed July 2003.

National Institute on Drug Abuse. 1998. Exploring the role of child abuse on later drug abuse. *NIDA Notes, 13(2).* Also available online: www.nida.nih.gov/NIDA_Notes/NNVol13N2/exploring.html. Accessed December 2003.

Pecora, P.J., Kessler, K.C., Williams, J., O'Brien, K., Downs, A.C., English, D., Hiripi, E., White, C.R., Wiggins, T., and Holmes, K. "Improving Family Foster Care: Findings from the Northwest Foster Care Alumni Study," (Seattle: Casey Family Programs, 2005). Available at www.casey.org

Perry, B. D. The neurodevelopmental impact of violence in childhood. In *Textbook of Child and Adolescent Forensic Psychiatry*, eds. D. Schetky and E. Benedek. Washington, DC: American Psychiatric Press, 2001. Also available online: http://www.childtrauma.org/ CTAMATERIALS/Vio_child.asp. Accessed February 2004.

———. 2002. Childhood experience and the expression of genetic potential: What childhood neglect tells us about nature and nurture. *Brain and Mind, 3,* 79–100.

Prevent Child Abuse America. 2001. Total estimated cost of child abuse and neglect in the United States. www.preventchildabuse. org/learn_more/ research_docs/cost_analysis.pdf. Accessed July 2003.

Prevent Child Abuse New York. 2001. Causes and consequences: The urgent need to prevent child abuse. www.pca-ny.org/causes.pdf. Accessed July 2003.

Psychjourney. Introduction to Buddhism series. 2006. http://www.psychjourney.com/Buddhism%20Series.htm. Retrieved June 19, 2009.Runyan, D. K., P. A. Curtis, W. M. Hunter, M. M. Black, J. B. Kotch, S. Bangdiwals, et al. 1998. Longscan: A consortium for longitudinal studies of maltreatment and the life course of children. *Aggression and Violent Behavior 3(3),* 275–285.

Shore, R. *Rethinking the Brain.* New York: Families and Work Institute, 1997.

Silverman, A. B., H. Z. Reinherz, R. M. Giaconia. 1996. The long-term sequel of child and adolescent abuse: A longitudinal community study. *Child Abuse and Neglect, 20(8),* 709–723.

Spirit of Vatican II: Buddhism – Buddhism and forgiveness. 2007.

http://josephsoleary.typepad.com/my_weblog/buddhism/index.html. Retrieved February 7, 2009.Teicher, M. D. 2000. Wounds that time won't heal: The neurobiology of child abuse. *Cerebrum: The Dana Forum on Brain Science, 2(4),* 50–67.

Thomlison, B. Risk and protective factors in child maltreatment. In *Risk and Resilience in Childhood: An Ecological Perspective,* ed. M. W. Fraser. Washington, DC: NASW Press, 1997.

United States Department of Health and Human Services. *Child Maltreatment 2001.* Washington, DC: Government Printing Office, 2003.

———. 2003. National survey of child and adolescent well-being: Baseline report for one-year-in-foster-care sample. http://www.acf. hhs.gov/programs/core/ongoing ng_research/afc/exec-sum_nscaw/exsum_nscaw.html. Accessed January 2004.

Widom, C. S. and M. G. Maxfield. *An Update on the 'Cycle of Violence.'* Washington, DC: National Institute of Justice, 2001.